ISBN EAN-13:   978-1-938117-7-49-7   [Soft cover Print Edition]

From the Publisher

GOLDEN WORDS UPON GOLDEN WORDS…FOR EVERY MUSLIM.

"Imaam al-Barbahaaree, may Allaah have mercy upon him said:

May Allaah have mercy upon you! Examine carefully the speech of everyone you hear from in your time particularly. So do not act in haste and do not enter into anything from it until you ask and see: Did any of the Companions of the Prophet, may Allaah's praise and salutations be upon him, speak about it, or did any of the scholars? So if you find a narration from them about it, cling to it, do not go beyond it for anything and do not give precedence to anything over it and thus fall into the Fire.

Explanation by Sheikh Saaleh al-Fauzaan, may Allaah preserve him:

'Do not be hasty in accepting as correct what you may hear from the people, especially in these later times. As now there are many who speak about so many various matters, issuing rulings and ascribing to themselves both knowledge and the right to speak. This is especially the case after the emergence and spread of new modern day media technologies. Such that everyone now can speak and bring forth that which is, in truth, worthless; by this, meaning words of no true value - speaking about whatever they wish in the name of knowledge and in the name of the religion of Islaam. It has even reached the point that you find the people of misguidance and the members of the various groups of misguidance and deviance from the religion speaking as well. Such individuals have now become those who speak in the name of the religion of Islaam through means such as the various satellite television channels. Therefore be very cautious!

It is upon you, oh Muslim, and upon you, oh student of knowledge, individually, to verify matters and not rush to embrace everything and anything you may hear. It is upon you to verify the truth of what you hear, asking, 'Who else also makes this same statement or claim?', 'Where did this thought or concept originate or come from?', 'Who is its reference or source authority?' Asking what are the evidences which support it from within the Book and the Sunnah? And inquiring where has the individual who is putting this forth studied and taken his knowledge from? From who has he studied the knowledge of Islaam?

Each of these matters requires verification through inquiry and investigation, especially in the present age and time. It is not every speaker who should rightly be considered a source of knowledge, even if he is well spoken and eloquent and can manipulate words captivating his listeners. Do not be taken in and accept him until you are aware of the degree and scope of what he possesses of knowledge and understanding. Perhaps someone's words may be few, but possess true understanding, and perhaps another will have a great deal of speech yet he is actually ignorant to such a degree that he doesn't actually possess anything of true understanding. Rather he only has the ability to enchant with his speech so that the people are deceived. Yet he puts forth the perception that he is a scholar, that he is someone of true understanding and comprehension, that he is a capable thinker, and so forth. Through such means and ways he is able to deceive and beguile the people, taking them away from the way of truth.

Therefore, what is to be given true consideration is not the amount of the speech put forth or that one can extensively discuss a subject. Rather, the criterion that is to be given consideration is what that speech contains within it of sound authentic knowledge, what it contains of the established and transmitted principles of Islaam. Perhaps a short or brief statement which is connected to or has a foundation in the established principles can be of greater benefit than a great deal of speech which simply rambles on, and through hearing you don't actually receive very much benefit from.

This is the reality which is present in our time; one sees a tremendous amount of speech which only possesses within it a small amount of actual knowledge. We see the presence of many speakers, yet few people of true understanding and comprehension.' "

[The eminent major scholar Sheikh Saaleh al-Fauzaan, may Allaah preserve him- 'A Valued Gift for the Reader Of Comments Upon the Book Sharh as-Sunnah', page 102-103]

❨ *Is not He better than your so-called gods, He Who originates creation and shall then repeat it, and Who provides for you from heaven and earth? Is there any god with Allaah? Say: 'Bring forth your proofs, if you are truthful.'* ❩ -(Surah an-Naml: 64)

Explanation: ❨ *Say: "Bring forth your proofs.."* ❩ This is a command for the Prophet, may Allaah's praise and salutation be upon him, to rebuke them immediately after they had put forward their own rebuke. Meaning: *'Say to them: bring your proof, whether it is an intellectual proof or a proof from transmitted knowledge, that would stand as evidence that there is another with Allaah, the Most Glorified and the Most Exalted'*. Additionally, it has been said that it means: *'Bring your proof that there is anyone other than Allaah, the Most High, who is capable of doing that which has been mentioned from His actions, the Most Glorified and the Most Exalted.'* ❨ *...if you are truthful.* ❩ meaning, in this claim. From this it is derived that a claim is not accepted unless clearly indicated by evidences."
[Tafseer al-'Aloosee: vol. 15, page 14]

Sheikh Rabee'a Ibn Hadee Umair al-Madkhalee, may Allaah preserve him said,

'It is possible for someone to simply say, *"So and so said such and such."* However we should say, *"Produce your proof."* So why did you not ask them for their proof by saying to them: *"Where was this said?"* Ask them questions such as this, as from your weapons are such questions as: *"Where is this from? From which book? From which cassette?..."* '
[The Overwhelming Falsehoods of 'Abdul-Lateef Bashmeel' page 14]

The guiding scholar Imaam Sheikh 'Abdul-'Azeez Ibn Abdullah Ibn Baaz, may Allaah have mercy upon him, said,

'It is not proper that any intelligent individual be misled or deceived by the great numbers from among people from the various countries who engage in such a practice. As the truth is not determined by the numerous people who engage in a matter, rather the truth is known by the Sharee'ah evidences. Just as Allaah the Most High says in Surah al-Baqarah, ❨ *And they say, "None shall enter Paradise unless he be a Jew or a Christian." These are only their own desires. Say "Produce your proof if you are truthful."* ❩-(Surah al-Baqarah: 111) And Allaah the Most High says ❨ *And if you obey most of those on the earth, they will mislead you far away from Allaah's path. They follow nothing but conjectures, and they do nothing but lie.* ❩-(Surah al-'Ana'an: 116)'
[Collection of Rulings and Various Statements of Sheikh Ibn Baaz -Vol. 1 page 85]

Sheikh Muhammad Ibn 'Abdul-Wahaab, may Allaah have mercy upon him, said,

'Additionally, verify that knowledge held regarding your beliefs, distinguishing between what is correct and false within it, coming to understand the various areas of knowledge of faith in Allaah alone and the required disbelief in all other objects of worship. You will certainly see various different matters which are called towards and enjoined; so if you see that a matter is in fact one coming from Allaah and His Messenger, then this is what is intended and is desired that you possess. Otherwise, Allaah has certainly given you that which enables you to distinguish between truth and falsehood, if Allaah so wills.

Moreover, this writing of mine- do not conceal it from the author of that work; rather present it to him. He may repent and affirm its truthfulness and then return to the guidance of Allaah, or perhaps if he says that he has a proof for his claims, even if that is only a single statement, or if he claims that within my statements there is something unsupported, then request his evidence for that assertion. After this if there is something which continues to cause uncertainty or is a problem for you, then refer it back to me, so that then you are aware of both his statement and mine in that issue. We ask Allaah to guide us, you, and all the Muslims to that which He loves and is pleased with.'

[Personal Letters of Sheikh Muhammad Ibn 'Abdul-Wahaab- Conclusion to Letter 20]

Sheikh 'Abdullah Ibn 'Abdur-Rahman Abu Bateen, may Allaah have mercy upon him, said,

'And for an individual, if it becomes clear to him that something is the truth, he should not turn away from it and or be discouraged simply due to the few people who agree with him and the many who oppose him in that, especially in these latter days of this present age.

If the ignorant one says: *"If this was the truth so and so and so and so would have been aware of it!"* However this is the very claim of the disbelievers, in their statement found in the Qur'aan ❰ ***If it had truly been good, they would not have preceded us to it!"*** ❱-(Surah al-Ahqaaf: 11) and in their statement ❰ ***Is it these whom Allaah has favored from amongst us?"*** ❱-(Surah al-Ana'am: 53). Yet certainly, as Alee Ibn Abee Taalib, may Allaah be pleased with him, stated *"Know the truth and then you will know it' people."* But for the one who generally stands upon confusion and uncertainty, then every doubt swirls around him. And if the majority of the people were in fact upon the truth today, then Islaam would not be considered strange, yet, by Allaah, it is today seen as the most strange of affairs!"

[Durar As-Sanneeyyah -vol. 10, page 400]

THE "30 DAYS OF GUIDANCE" SERIES

The goal of the "*30 Days of Guidance*" book series is to better enable us, as worshipers of Allaah, to embody and reflect in the various different areas of life for a Muslim, our connection and adherence to the believer's path of the first three believing generations. Many Muslims, due to lacking opportunities to study consistently and be cultivated at the feet of noble steadfast scholars, have an inconsistency they themselves recognize an inconsistency between the clear path of Islaam of the first Muslims, which they have connected themselves to, and what they have actually been successful in making a daily reality in their practice of Islaam. Sheikh Saaleh Ibn al-Fauzaan, may Allaah preserve him, explained the importance of striving to rectify this,

"... For the one who proceeds upon the methodology of the best generations even if that is during the very last days of the existence of earth, then he is safe, saved, and protected from entering the Hellfire. As Allaah, the Most Glorified and the Most Exalted, said, **And the first to embrace Islaam of the Muhaajiroon (those who migrated from Makkah to Al-Madinah) and the Ansaar (the citizens of Al-Madinah who helped and gave aid to the Muhaajiroon) and also those who followed them exactly (in faith). Allaah is well-pleased with them as they are well-pleased with Him. He has prepared for them Gardens under which rivers flow (Paradise), to dwell therein forever. That is the supreme success.** *—(Surah Al-Tawbah:100)*

*So Allaah, the Most Exalted, the Most Magnificent, has included and described them as those who follow Muhaajiroon and the Ansaar, upon a condition, "**who followed them exactly (in faith).**" Meaning truly followed them with precision and integrity, not merely putting forth a claim or outwardly attributing or attaching themselves to them without actually realizing their guidance. This is true whether that shortfall is caused by ignorance or by the following of desires. Not everyone who attributes himself to the first three generations is true in his assertion unless he follows them precisely and with integrity. This is in fact a condition, a condition placed by Allaah, the Most Glorified and the Most Exalted. The wording "**exactly (in faith).** meaning precisely, with integrity, as well as entirely.*

What is required in truly following them is that you study the methodology of the Salaf, that you understand it, and that you are firmly attached to it. But as for individuals who simply attribute themselves to them, while they do not really understand their methodology nor their way, then this does not really benefit them with anything, and does not actually help them in anyway. Such people are not from those upon the way of the Salaf and should not be considered Salafees. Because they are not following the first generations precisely with integrity, as indeed Allaah, the Most Glorified and the Most Exalted, has placed this as the condition for their following of them to be true.

....The one who proceeds upon the methodology of the Salaf must have two characteristics, as we have previously mentioned. Firstly, actually understanding the methodology of the first generations, and the second matter is adhering firmly to it, even when it causes him hardship and discomfort. As he will certainly encounter a great deal of that from those who oppose this path of guidance. He will encounter harassment. He will encounter stubbornness. He will encounter false accusations. He will face having directed towards him evil names and false labels. However, he must remain patient in the face of this, as he is convinced and satisfied with what he stands upon. He should be not shaken or troubled in the face of a whirlwind of difficulties. He should not be affected or changed by what he encounters of different trials, but remains patient when facing them until he meets his Lord.

Accordingly, one must firstly learn the methodology of the first three generation, and then follow it exactly with integrity, while being patient with what you encounter from the people due to this adherence. Yet this in and of itself is also not enough, it is additionally necessary to spread the methodology of the first generations. It is required to invite the people to Allaah and invite them to the way of the Salaf, to explain it to the people and spread this way among them. The one who does this is Salafee in reality and truth. But as for the one who claims Salafeeyah, yet he does not truly understand the methodology of the Salaf, or he does indeed understand it yet fails to truly follow it, but simply follows what the people are upon, or merely follows what happens to agree with his desires. This one is not Salafee, even if he calls and labels himself that.

This fact demands from us that we place great importance in fully comprehending the way of the first generations and studying their methodology in beliefs, character, and actions in every environment and situation. As the path and methodology of the first three generations is that methodology upon which the Messenger of Allaah, may the praise and salutations be upon him, was upon, and is that way which those who follow the best of generations and walk upon their path, will proceed upon until the Final Hour is established....

...As such, it is required that the one who claims this way, or connects himself to the Salaf make this descriptive name a reality and make his attachment to them something which truly reflects the way of the first generations in beliefs, and in statements, and in actions, and in general dealings. So that he may be a true Salafee and that he may be a righteous example to others and someone who sincerely reflects the way of the righteous first generations of Islaam." [1]

We ask Allaah for success in each of our efforts to both learn and reflect the clear path of the first three generations, in every area of our individual lives, the lives of our spouses, and the lives of our children. And the success is from Allaah.

---

[1]   From the lecture "Salafeeyah, Its Reality And Its Characteristics" http://www.alfawzan.af.org.sa/

30 Days of Guidance:
Cultivating The Character & Behavior of Islaam

A Short Journey through the work al-Adab al-Mufrad
with Sheikh Zayd Ibn Muhammad Ibn Haadee al-Madkhalee

[Exercise Workbook]

Compiled and Translated by:
Abu Sukhailah Khalil Ibn-Abelahyi

Student name:_____

Date started:_____

Date completed:_____

Online login:_____

Online pass:_____

How to use this Exercise Workbook

This workbook can be used to make it simpler for the one administering a study circle to check all exercise homewor from the answer key which is available at the back of the [Self-Study / Teachers Edition].The exercise workbooks can be collected after class or at another convenient time for student work to be checked before proceeding to the next day.

A small marking area has been added for indicating correct and incorrect answers at the bottom of each page. Depending on question type , there is a [/1] or [/3] for recording the number of correct answers out of total answers on that specific page. Partial scores can be given for essay answers that may not completely fulfill the needed answer, and then clarifying notes added in the teacher notes section below the same essay answer area. In addition, there is also an final total correct area i.e. =[/15] at the end of each day's section for recording the total number of correct answers for each individual day's exercises.

SCORING EACH DAYS EXERCISE ASSESSMENT TOTAL

Multiply the total points of correct answers (max. 15) times (X) 6.7 for score out of 100.

Sheikh Muhammad Ibn Saaleh al-'Utheimeen, may Allaah have mercy upon him, said,

"Also from your contemplating Allaah is that you do so with regard to your inner secrets and what is in your heart. Look to what is in your heart! Associating partners with Allaah, showing off, deviations, jealousy, hatred and dislike displayed towards the Muslims, love of the disbelievers and other such things that Allaah is not pleased with. Scrutinize and be attentive to your heart, for Allaah has said, ❴ ***Indeed We created man, and We know what his own self whispers to him.*** ❵ -(Surah Qaaf:16)

So contemplate Allaah in these three places in your actions, your statements, and within your heart so that your contemplation may be complete. This is why, when the Prophet, may Allaah's praise and salutations be upon him, was asked about *Ihsaan*, he replied, ***{... that you worship Allaah as if you see Him, and if you do not see Him, then indeed He sees you}***. Worship Allaah as if you see Him and witness Him with your eye, and if you cannot do so as if you were seeing Him then worship Him on a station below this by remembering that, indeed, He sees you. So the first station is to worship Him out of hope and desire. The next is to worship Him out of fear and awe this is why he said, ***{and if you do not see Him, then indeed He sees you.}*** .

As such, it is necessary for a person to contemplate His Lord and that he know that Allaah is watching over him. Anything that you say or do or keep secret, Allaah, Exalted is He, knows it."

(From his explanation of 'Riyaadh as-Saaliheen' may Allaah have abundant mercy upon him)

TABLE OF CONTENTS

DAY 1: DO YOU UNDERSTAND THE NATURE OF ISLAAM?

TEST YOUR UNDERSTANDING:

3min

TRUE & FALSE QUESTIONS

[Circle the correct letter for each individual sentence from today's content.]

01. The Prophet Muhammad called to a different religion than the [T / F]
    religion of Ibraaheem, may the praise and salutations of Allaah
    be upon them.

02. Allaah is pleased with our worship as long as most of what we [T / F]
    do as worship is for Allaah.

03. The revealed guidance which was given to different messengers [T / F]
    shared some fundamental aspects and differed in other
    fundamental aspects.

6min

FILL IN THE BLANK QUESTIONS

[Enter the correct individual words to complete the sentences from today's content.]

04. _____, which is mentioned in the verse in the lesson, refers to
    the religion of Ibraheem.

05. Allaah is the only One deserving and worthy of all forms of _____.

06. Any _____that does not stand upon the foundation of
    establishing the worship of Allaah alone is in fact a false _____.

INTERACTIVE QUESTIONS & EXERCISES

COMPREHENSIVE UNDERSTANDING QUESTIONS

07. In our daily lives, how can we know what Allaah loves and what Allaah hates?

TEACHER NOTES / CORRECTIONS

✽[/ 3]

7-12min

08. Give an example of a false practice of any religion that directs an act of worship to the creation, instead of directing it to Allaah alone.

_____
_____
_____
_____
_____
_____
_____
_____
_____
_____
_____
_____
_____
_____
_____
_____
_____
_____
_____
_____
_____
_____
_____
_____
_____
_____

TEACHER NOTES / CORRECTIONS

_____
_____
_____
_____
_____

7-12 min

09. List five deeds which are acts of obedience to Allaah which we should do as part of our worship of Allaah alone.

TEACHER NOTES / CORRECTIONS

*[/3]=[/15]

TEST YOUR UNDERSTANDING:

TRUE & FALSE QUESTIONS

[Circle the correct letter for each individual sentence from today's content.]

3 min

01. The meaning of being wealthy in Islaam is not restricted to [T / F] financial and material wealth.

02. It is not required that a Muslim be thankful for that wealth he [T / F] worked for and earned with his own hands.

03. It is not obligatory to obey the ruler in what is permissible [T / F] unless you chose and selected him yourself.

FILL IN THE BLANK QUESTIONS

[Enter the correct individual words to complete the sentences from today's content.]

6 min

04. One aspect of being wealthy is having enough food for a _____.

05. It is a tremendous blessing from Allaah for a Muslim to live in a land where he is secure in his _____, _____, _____, and generally secure from being _____.

06. What is enough for an individual of wealth, is what is enough for his _____ needs.

7-12min

COMPREHENSIVE UNDERSTANDING QUESTIONS

07. Give an example of those people who do not have this correct balanced understanding and practice of having wealth in Islaam, either in terms of being excessive or in terms of being deficient.

TEACHER NOTES / CORRECTIONS

*[/3]

08. Name three Muslim countries in which either today (or recently) many of the Muslims lacked all of these various aspects of wealth

TEACHER NOTES / CORRECTIONS

09. Why is it important that the Muslims do not make the seeking of wealth and living comfortably their primary focus and occupation?

TEACHER NOTES / CORRECTIONS

✻[/ 3]=[/ 15]

TEST YOUR UNDERSTANDING:

TRUE & FALSE QUESTIONS

[Circle the correct letter for each individual sentence from today's content.]

3min

01. The person who spends a good deal of money helping the   [T / F]
    Muslims is someone who is wealthy..

02. Dissatisfaction and impatience with the amount of income   [T / F]
    that someone has been blessed with can lead a Muslim towards
    impermissible ways of making money.

03. Remembering that his income and livelihood is something   [T / F]
    decreed by Allaah leads a Muslim towards simply waiting for
    that to reach him.

FILL IN THE BLANK QUESTIONS

[Enter the correct individual words to complete the sentences from today's content.]

6min

04. Generosity means to spend in a _____ way and doing so liberally in
    its _____ place.

05. A Muslim is accountable for knowing whether his _____ comes
    from that which is _____ to him or that which has been
    _____ to him.

06. True wealth is the wealth regarding _____, meaning that
    a person be _____ with what Allaah has decreed for him of
    _____ and wealth.

COMPREHENSIVE UNDERSTANDING QUESTIONS

7-12 min

07.   What are three specific beneficial ways that we can be generous to others and spend our wealth in a way pleasing to Allaah?

_____

_____

_____

_____

_____

_____

_____

_____

_____

_____

_____

_____

_____

_____

_____

_____

_____

_____

_____

_____

TEACHER NOTES / CORRECTIONS

_____

_____

_____

_____

_____

✻[/ 3]

08. How should we view the various permissible material possessions that we acquire and use in this world? Give a specific example.

TEACHER NOTES / CORRECTIONS

09. Generally, what inner condition does our praising of Allaah in our speech and actions for the good we have received reflect?

_____

_____

_____

_____

_____

_____

_____

_____

_____

_____

_____

_____

_____

_____

_____

_____

_____

_____

_____

_____

_____

_____

TEACHER NOTES / CORRECTIONS

_____

_____

_____

_____

_____

*[/ 3]=[/ 15]

TEST YOUR UNDERSTANDING:

TRUE & FALSE QUESTIONS

[Circle the correct letter for each individual sentence from today's content.]

01. A Muslim should not have any concern for worldly affairs.   [T / F]

02. It is possible to have a good end to this life.   [T / F]

03. It is not a significant issue to only give minimal attention to   [T / F] what brings success in the Hereafter, as indeed Allaah has told us that He is very merciful.

3min

FILL IN THE BLANK QUESTIONS

[Enter the correct individual words to complete the sentences from today's content.]

04. A _____ benefits the believers.

05. There is no general contradiction between taking care of one's needs in this _____ and putting forth deeds and efforts for the _____ _____..

06. We should always remember that _____ is something close to us, and act accordingly.

6min

COMPREHENSIVE UNDERSTANDING QUESTIONS

7-12 min

DAY - 04

07. Was the Prophet, may the praise and salutations of Allaah be upon him, telling the Companion, may Allaah be pleased with him, to stop fixing his home? What did he intend by his words?

_____
_____
_____
_____
_____
_____
_____
_____
_____
_____
_____
_____
_____
_____
_____
_____
_____
_____
_____
_____
_____
_____
_____
_____
_____

TEACHER NOTES / CORRECTIONS

_____
_____
_____
_____

*[/ 3]

08. Give two examples of how people waste their time and/or their wealth in pursuing things that only benefit them in this world.

TEACHER NOTES / CORRECTIONS

09. Why is success in the Hereafter more important than having everything that we want in this world?

_____
_____
_____
_____
_____
_____
_____
_____
_____
_____
_____
_____
_____
_____
_____
_____
_____
_____
_____
_____
_____
_____
_____
_____
_____

TEACHER NOTES / CORRECTIONS

_____
_____
_____
_____
_____

✱[/ 3]=[/ 15]

DAY - 05 TEST YOUR UNDERSTANDING:

TRUE & FALSE QUESTIONS

[Circle the correct letter for each individual sentence from today's content.]

3 min

01. A Muslim should continually seek the good of this world in   [T / F]
their priorities and practices

02. There is no benefit in a Muslim earning anything above his   [T / F]
daily needs.

03. The benefit of income earned in a permissible way ends when   [T / F]
you die.

FILL IN THE BLANK QUESTIONS

[Enter the correct individual words to complete the sentences from today's content.]

6 min

04. We should give attention to the _____ that Allaah has given us,
to make it _____.

05. It is prohibited to _____ one's wealth, and _____ your money.

06. Every soul will be recompensed for what they _____ according to
their _____.

COMPREHENSIVE UNDERSTANDING QUESTIONS

7-12min

DAY - 05

07. List three ways that you would like to be able to spend any permissible saved money in the future.

_____

_____

_____

_____

_____

_____

_____

_____

_____

_____

_____

_____

_____

_____

_____

_____

_____

_____

_____

_____

_____

TEACHER NOTES / CORRECTIONS

_____

_____

_____

_____

✳[/ 3]

08. List three possible things that Muslims today waste or squander their money upon without realizing it.

TEACHER NOTES / CORRECTIONS

09. List three ways that a Muslim who is moderate in seeking wealth can financially benefit the community that he lives in.

_____

_____

_____

_____

_____

_____

_____

_____

_____

_____

_____

_____

_____

_____

_____

_____

_____

_____

_____

_____

_____

TEACHER NOTES / CORRECTIONS

_____

_____

_____

_____

_____

*[/ 3]=[/ 15]

TEST YOUR UNDERSTANDING:

DAY - 06

TRUE & FALSE QUESTIONS

[Circle the correct letter for each individual sentence from today's content.]

3min

01. Everyone who goes through a hardship achieves some good and has his sins removed. [T / F]

02. A Muslim should be satisfied with the hardships that Allaah has decreed for him. [T / F]

03. If a Muslim is blessed with something all he needs to do is be thankful for it. [T / F]

FILL IN THE BLANK QUESTIONS

[Enter the correct individual words to complete the sentences from today's content.]

6min

04. Whenever a believer _____, this wipes away from him some of his _____ and _____.

05. When a believer is blessed with something of _____ he should inwardly be _____ to Allaah.

06. When a believer is _____ with something of goodness he should use that blessing for something Allaah is _____ with.

COMPREHENSIVE UNDERSTANDING QUESTIONS

7-12 min

DAY - 06

07.   Why is it the case that anything a believer encounters can be a source of good for him?

_____

_____

_____

_____

_____

_____

_____

_____

_____

_____

_____

_____

_____

_____

_____

_____

_____

_____

_____

_____

_____

_____

_____

_____

_____

TEACHER NOTES / CORRECTIONS

_____

_____

_____

_____

*[/3]

7-12 min

08.   Give three examples of hardships coming from others that Muslims might encounter.

_____

_____

_____

_____

_____

_____

_____

_____

_____

_____

_____

_____

_____

_____

_____

_____

_____

_____

_____

_____

_____

_____

_____

_____

_____

_____

TEACHER NOTES / CORRECTIONS

_____

_____

_____

_____

09. List five specific ways or examples that a blessing Allaah has given you could be used in a good way.

7-12 min

_____

_____

_____

_____

_____

_____

_____

_____

_____

_____

_____

_____

_____

_____

_____

_____

_____

_____

_____

_____

_____

_____

_____

_____

_____

_____

TEACHER NOTES / CORRECTIONS

_____

_____

_____

_____

_____

✱[/ 3]=[/ 15]

TEST YOUR UNDERSTANDING:

TRUE & FALSE QUESTIONS

[Circle the correct letter for each individual sentence from today's content.]

3min

01. Good character is something which is optional and not [T / F] connected to the rights of people.

02. Good character benefits a Muslim in both the Hereafter and [T / F] this world.

03. Sins do not have lesser matters which lead to them. [T / F]

FILL IN THE BLANK QUESTIONS

[Enter the correct individual words to complete the sentences from today's content.]

6min

04. Two things which lead many people to enter Hellfire are the _____ and the _____.

05. Two things which lead many people to enter Paradise are having _____ and good _____.

06. The meaning of having taqwa is the performance of the _____ of Allaah and the staying away from the _____ of Allaah.

COMPREHENSIVE UNDERSTANDING QUESTIONS

7-12min

07. What are some of the sins and transgressions specific to our modern age which are related to speaking with the tongue?

DAY - 07

_____

_____

_____

_____

_____

_____

_____

_____

_____

_____

_____

_____

_____

_____

_____

_____

_____

_____

_____

_____

_____

_____

_____

_____

TEACHER NOTES / CORRECTIONS

_____

_____

_____

_____

✻[/ 3]

7-12 min

08.   What are some of the challenges that Muslims face today related to preserving their private parts from sin?

_____
_____
_____
_____
_____
_____
_____
_____
_____
_____
_____
_____
_____
_____
_____
_____
_____
_____
_____
_____
_____
_____
_____
_____
_____

TEACHER NOTES / CORRECTIONS

_____
_____
_____
_____
_____
_____

09. List five acts or behaviors which might be considered part of having good character, which you believe are important.

DAY - 07

7-12 min

TEACHER NOTES / CORRECTIONS

*[/3]=[/15]

TEST YOUR UNDERSTANDING:

TRUE & FALSE QUESTIONS

[Circle the correct letter for each individual sentence from today's content.]

01. A Muslim will be with those he loves only if he reaches their   [T / F]
    level of goodness and worship.

02. The most important and essential love we should have is the   [T / F]
    love of Allaah.

03. The love of Allaah is connected to other aspects of required   [T / F]
    love towards His creation.

FILL IN THE BLANK QUESTIONS

[Enter the correct individual words to complete the sentences from today's content.]

04. The most trustworthy handhold upon *emaan* or faith is to _____ for
    the sake of Allaah and to _____ for the sake of Allaah.

05. Every Muslim should love Allaah with a love that is _____ and
    worthy of His _____ and exaltedness.

06. The love of the Messenger of Allaah, may the praise and salutations be
    upon him, is an _____.

COMPREHENSIVE UNDERSTANDING QUESTIONS

7-12 min

07.   What are some of the things that the people love instead of loving Allaah?

DAY - 08

TEACHER NOTES / CORRECTIONS

*[/ 3]

7-12 min

08.   How is our love of the righteous worshipers connected to our love of Allaah?

DAY - 08

TEACHER NOTES / CORRECTIONS

09. What are three separate mentioned reasons why we should love the Messenger of Allaah, may the praise and salutations of Allaah be upon him?

TEACHER NOTES / CORRECTIONS

TEST YOUR UNDERSTANDING:

TRUE & FALSE QUESTIONS

[Circle the correct letter for each individual sentence from today's content.]

3min

01. The souls of the Muslims upon the Sunnah unite because they   [T / F]
    understand the truth, act according to the truth, and call the
    people to the truth.

02. If souls are similar in their orientation, then people become   [T / F]
    acquainted and gravitate together whenever possible.

03. The attraction or separation of souls is according to what Allaah   [T / F]
    created them upon of general fundamental orientation.

FILL IN THE BLANK QUESTIONS

[Enter the correct individual words to complete the sentences from today's content.]

6min

04. _____ is the greatest of the sins against Allaah.

05. Freeing yourself from _____ in Islaam is being truly merciful to
    your own _____.

06. _____ souls gravitate towards the other _____ souls
    among them, and the _____ souls gravitate towards the other
    _____ souls among them.

COMPREHENSIVE UNDERSTANDING QUESTIONS

7-12 min

07. Give a practical example of how souls who unite upon the truth come to agree and work together upon something of good.

DAY - 09

TEACHER NOTES / CORRECTIONS

7-12 min

08. Give a practical example of how souls that differ, such as those who adhere to the Sunnah and those separate souls upon innovation, cannot agree and work on a matter in which they differ.

TEACHER NOTES / CORRECTIONS

09. What are two discussed ways that the person who stands upon the Sunnah is known to be merciful?

TEACHER NOTES / CORRECTIONS

TEST YOUR UNDERSTANDING:

TRUE & FALSE QUESTIONS

[Circle the correct letter for each individual sentence from today's content.]

3min

DAY - 10

01. It is never permissible to mention an individual's possible evil, as this is impermissible backbiting.   [T / F]

02. A Muslim does not need to bother to protect himself from someone's evil, as everything is decreed.   [T / F]

03. The best way to change any situation is to supplicate and then wait patiently.   [T / F]

FILL IN THE BLANK QUESTIONS

[Enter the correct individual words to complete the sentences from today's content.]

6min

04. The people of evil have no _____ about who is affected when they spread their _____ among people.

05. A Muslim _____ himself from _____ in a good way that does not cause him to fall into doing what is _____ in Islaam.

06. If you see something that requires that you point it out or criticize it, then try to _____ it with _____.

COMPREHENSIVE UNDERSTANDING QUESTIONS

7-12 min

07. Give an example of responding in a good way to someone who comes up to you and says bad things about Muslims in general.

DAY - 10

TEACHER NOTES / CORRECTIONS

*[/3]

08. Name a specific modern sect, group, or organization that the scholars have spoken about indicating their mistakes, in order to warn the Muslims from errors in understanding and practice.

DAY - 10

TEACHER NOTES / CORRECTIONS

09. Give a specific example of when a Muslim should proceed carefully and with deliberation in relation to a problem they encounter with others.

TEACHER NOTES / CORRECTIONS

TEST YOUR UNDERSTANDING:

TRUE & FALSE QUESTIONS

[Circle the correct letter for each individual sentence from today's content.]

3min

DAY - 11

01. The giving of the greeting of salaams contains good for our hearts.   [T / F]

02. The Prophet and his companions frequently made supplications to Allaah.   [T / F]

03. There are no conditions for a supplication to be accepted.   [T / F]

FILL IN THE BLANK QUESTIONS

[Enter the correct individual words to complete the sentences from today's content.]

6min

04. From the _____ of success in making a supplication is that one is not _____ in expecting a result.

05. Supplication is from the best of acts of _____ which are easy for us to do, and which bring _____ to our hearts.

06. We should strive to _____ the giving of the salaam in every _____ we find ourselves in.

COMPREHENSIVE UNDERSTANDING QUESTIONS

7-12min

07. What are some of the negative consequences of neglecting to spread the greetings of salaams among the Muslims?

DAY - 11

_____
_____
_____
_____
_____
_____
_____
_____
_____
_____
_____
_____
_____
_____
_____
_____
_____
_____
_____
_____
_____
_____

TEACHER NOTES / CORRECTIONS

_____
_____
_____
_____
_____

✳[/ 3]

08.   Describe two different reasons why someone supplication would not be responded to.

_____

_____

_____

_____

_____

_____

_____

_____

_____

_____

_____

_____

_____

_____

_____

_____

_____

_____

_____

_____

_____

_____

_____

_____

TEACHER NOTES / CORRECTIONS

_____

_____

_____

_____

_____

_____

09. Give an example of an authentic transmitted supplication that we make when performing ritual prayer.

TEACHER NOTES / CORRECTIONS

*[/3]=[/15]

DAY 12: DO YOU KNOW THE BEST OF SUPPLICATIONS?

TEST YOUR UNDERSTANDING:

TRUE & FALSE QUESTIONS

[Circle the correct letter for each individual sentence from today's content.]

3 min

01. A Muslim should seek the good of this world as well as the next. [T / F]

02. There is no benefit in using the supplications which are [T / F] transmitted, just our own personal supplications.

03. There are several well-known specific books which can be used [T / F] to learn the supplications found in the authentic Sunnah.

FILL IN THE BLANK QUESTIONS

[Enter the correct individual words to complete the sentences from today's content.]

6 min

04. The tremendous book, "al-Adhkaar", was collected by Imaam _____, may Allaah mercy upon him.

05. One of the praiseworthy characteristics _____ to the Prophet, was the ability to speak _____.

06. Using _____ supplications can only _____ the believer in good.

[/ 6]✳

COMPREHENSIVE UNDERSTANDING QUESTIONS

7-12 min

07.   What is one benefit of making a comprehensive supplication such as the one
       mentioned in the lesson?

_____

_____

_____

_____

_____

_____

_____

_____

_____

_____

_____

_____

_____

_____

_____

_____

_____

_____

DAY - 12

TEACHER NOTES / CORRECTIONS

_____

_____

_____

_____

✳[/ 3]

08. Give general examples of one matter that a Muslim might supplicate for seeking good in this world, and a different second matter that a Muslim might supplicate for seeking the good of the Hereafter.

DAY - 12

TEACHER NOTES / CORRECTIONS

09. Give two specific examples within our daily lives where we could use specific supplications from the authentic Sunnah.

7-12 min

TEACHER NOTES / CORRECTIONS

＊[/3]=[/15]

TEST YOUR UNDERSTANDING:

TRUE & FALSE QUESTIONS

[Circle the correct letter for each individual sentence from today's content.]

3 min

01.   The things we listen to are not important and don't really affect   [T / F]
      us.

02.   If we use our bodies for good we benefit in this world and in   [T / F]
      the Hereafter.

03.   It is important to ask Allaah to assist us in keeping ourselves   [T / F]
      away from the evil our bodies may commit.

FILL IN THE BLANK QUESTIONS

[Enter the correct individual words to complete the sentences from today's content.]

6 min

04.   Every general individual does some _____ deeds but he also does some
      _____ deeds.

05.   Evil deeds may be those which are related to the _____ or may be what
      are related to the ____ _____ and to the _____.

06.   It is impermissible to look at people who are improperly dressed whether
      this is through your _____ and the _____, or actually out in
      the _____ or in the _____.

DAY - 13

COMPREHENSIVE UNDERSTANDING QUESTIONS

7-12 min

07.   Give an example of two ways someone can use his hearing to benefit himself, and two ways that are sinful and cause Allaah's anger.

DAY - 13

TEACHER NOTES / CORRECTIONS

*[/ 3]

08. Give an example of two ways someone can use his eyesight to benefit himself, and two ways that are sinful and cause Allaah's anger.

_____

_____

_____

_____

_____

_____

_____

_____

_____

_____

_____

_____

_____

_____

_____

_____

_____

_____

_____

TEACHER NOTES / CORRECTIONS

_____

_____

_____

_____

_____

09. Give an example of two ways someone can use his tongue to benefit himself, and two ways that are sinful and cause Allaah's anger.

TEACHER NOTES / CORRECTIONS

*[/3]=[/15]

TEST YOUR UNDERSTANDING:

TRUE & FALSE QUESTIONS

[Circle the correct letter for each individual sentence from today's content.]

3 min

01. Not every supplication is responded to immediately. [T / F]

02. It is not really important to supplicate about the personal [T / F]
     shortcomings and faults mentioned, but you should work to
     fix them.

03. It is permissible to perform the witr or salaat in a number of [T / F]
     different ways.

DAY - 14

FILL IN THE BLANK QUESTIONS

[Enter the correct individual words to complete the sentences from today's content.]

6 min

04. The Prophet, may the praise and salutations of Allaah be upon him,
     said {_____ to Allaah while you are _____ of Him
     _____ to you.}

05. The best form of ritual prayer at _____ is performed after the one
     _____ for a period, and it is named tahajjud.

06. It is permissible to perform _____ by a single _____.

COMPREHENSIVE UNDERSTANDING QUESTIONS

7-12 min

07. What is one of the greatest merits of a person taking time to supplicate in the later part of the night?

_____

_____

_____

_____

_____

_____

_____

_____

_____

DAY - 14

_____

_____

_____

_____

_____

_____

_____

_____

_____

_____

_____

_____

_____

TEACHER NOTES / CORRECTIONS

_____

_____

_____

_____

✳[/ 3]

08. Is there any benefit in using those supplications which mention faults that someone doesn't personally have? Explain your answer.

7-12min

DAY - 14

TEACHER NOTES / CORRECTIONS

/3]*

09. List as many different forms of worship that have been mentioned which are considered part of "standing at night".

TEACHER NOTES / CORRECTIONS

*[/3]=[/15]

TEST YOUR UNDERSTANDING:

TRUE & FALSE QUESTIONS

[Circle the correct letter for each individual sentence from today's content.]

3min

01. There are some trials and tribulations that may overcome or [T / F] overwhelm a Muslim in remaining steadfast.

02. The people of the Sunnah do not have enemies from among [T / F] those who claim to follow Islaam.

03. A Muslim whose knowledge is sound and emaan is strong [T / F] is affected and sympathetic when something happens to his Muslim brother.

DAY - 15

FILL IN THE BLANK QUESTIONS

[Enter the correct individual words to complete the sentences from today's content.]

6min

04. From the causes of being miserable is _____ into _____ actions and _____ acts of _____.

05. There are some trials and afflictions which may be _____ your personal _____ to bear.

06. When a Muslim makes a supplication, he should not be _____ or hasty in expecting a _____.

COMPREHENSIVE UNDERSTANDING QUESTIONS

7-12 min

07.   List three of the painful trials mentioned which a Muslim should seek refuge in Allaah from.

DAY - 15

TEACHER NOTES / CORRECTIONS

✳[/ 3]

08. List two sinful actions a Muslim might fall into, and two beneficial actions a Muslim might abandon if they were put to trial by the causes of being "miserable", as defined in the lesson.

DAY - 15

TEACHER NOTES / CORRECTIONS

09. List two possible things which might cause the external enemies of the Muslims to gloat over them.

7-12 min

DAY - 15

TEACHER NOTES / CORRECTIONS

*[/3]=[/15]

TEST YOUR UNDERSTANDING:

TRUE & FALSE QUESTIONS

[Circle the correct letter for each individual sentence from today's content.]

3min

01. The supplication of the traveler is responded to by Allaah no [T / F] matter why he is traveling.

02. Miraculous occurrences only happened to the prophets and [T / F] messengers.

03. Supplicating for our absent Muslim brothers assists in the [T / F] purifying of our hearts.

DAY - 16

FILL IN THE BLANK QUESTIONS

[Enter the correct individual words to complete the sentences from today's content.]

6min

04. It is not _____ that a believer _____ and _____ _____ in supplicating for his believing brothers and sisters.

05. It is _____ in the Sharee'ah to request supplications be made for you from _____ Muslims that you know to be _____ and good people.

06. An individual who was traveling for a _____ or _____ purpose is not considered from those whose supplication is definitely _____ to.

COMPREHENSIVE UNDERSTANDING QUESTIONS

7-12 min

07.   List three things that you believe are important to make supplication for in regard to your present or future children.

_____

_____

_____

_____

_____

_____

_____

_____

_____

_____

_____

_____

_____

DAY - 16

_____

_____

_____

_____

_____

_____

_____

_____

_____

TEACHER NOTES / CORRECTIONS

_____

_____

_____

_____

✶[/ 3]

08. List three possible ways in which a Muslim might be oppressive towards his Muslim brother.

TEACHER NOTES / CORRECTIONS

09. Discuss another merit or excellent characteristic of the Companion of the Messenger of Allaah, Abu Hurairah, may Allaah be pleased with him.

7-12 min

DAY - 16

_____

| TEACHER NOTES / CORRECTIONS |

✻[/3]=[/15]

TEST YOUR UNDERSTANDING:

TRUE & FALSE QUESTIONS

[Circle the correct letter for each individual sentence from today's content.]

3min

01. We can pray the salaat or ritual prayer in that way that seems good to us. [T / F]

02. Kindness and listening to your parents is something which is a recommended action that someone should consider doing. [T / F]

03. Jihaad, as found in the guidance of the Qur'aan and authentic Sunnah, has different levels with different priorities. [T / F]

DAY - 17

6min

FILL IN THE BLANK QUESTIONS

[Enter the correct individual words to complete the sentences from today's content.]

04. Jihaad should be conducted under the _____ of the _____ ruler.

05. There is nothing to _____ someone who committed a transgression from sincerely _____ .

06. One of the _____ actions to bring a person near to _____ is dutifulness to his _____.

COMPREHENSIVE UNDERSTANDING QUESTIONS

7-12min

07. Give three specific examples of ways that you can show kindness and obedience to your parents.

DAY - 17

TEACHER NOTES / CORRECTIONS

✳[/ 3]

7-12min

08. Give two specific examples of common misconceptions that Muslims have today regarding jihaad.

_____

_____

_____

_____

_____

_____

_____

_____

_____

_____

_____

_____

_____

_____

_____

_____

_____

_____

_____

_____

_____

_____

_____

TEACHER NOTES / CORRECTIONS

_____

_____

_____

_____

_____

09. What is the worst sin that someone can commit? Explain how a person would repent from it.

TEACHER NOTES / CORRECTIONS

*[/ 3]=[/ 15]

TEST YOUR UNDERSTANDING:

TRUE & FALSE QUESTIONS

[Circle the correct letter for each individual sentence from today's content.]

3min

01. Each of us is only responsible for ourselves. [T / F]

02. The goal of hanging up a whip in your house is to be able to [T / F] use it for any mistake large or small.

03. A Muslim father is only responsible for giving his children a [T / F] place to live and food until they grow up.

FILL IN THE BLANK QUESTIONS

[Enter the correct individual words to complete the sentences from today's content.]

DAY - 18

6min

04. A father has a _____ towards his children for their _____, _____ them, and teaching them what is correct.

05. The Muslim woman should gain the experience and _____ of her responsibility in order to _____ what she's been _____ with in her household.

06. No one who has reached the age of _____ is free from having a responsibility to at least _____.

COMPREHENSIVE UNDERSTANDING QUESTIONS

7-12min

07. Give three examples of possible ways a Muslim should fulfill the responsibility he has towards his own self.

DAY - 18

TEACHER NOTES / CORRECTIONS

✳[/ 3]

08. Give three examples of possible ways a Muslim could neglect the responsibility he has to himself.

TEACHER NOTES / CORRECTIONS

09. Give three examples of three matters which the Muslim leader in a Muslim country has a responsibility for.

7-12min

DAY - 18

TEACHER NOTES / CORRECTIONS

*[/3]=[/15]

TEST YOUR UNDERSTANDING:

TRUE & FALSE QUESTIONS

[Circle the correct letter for each individual sentence from today's content.]

01. The Muslim woman who is thankful to her husband is also [T / F] being thankful to Allaah.

02. What is due upon our neighbors is only that we do good [T / F] towards them when able to.

03. The good deeds that you do can always wipe out any bad deeds [T / F] and transgressions.

FILL IN THE BLANK QUESTIONS

[Enter the correct individual words to complete the sentences from today's content.]

04. Human beings are _____ prone to making _____.

05. The Prophet, may the praise and salutations of Allaah be upon him, considered _____ as a lesser form of _____ , which is a sin but does not take you out of Islaam.

06. A Muslim may not be _____ from Hellfire by their many _____ deeds, if, in addition to doing them, they also _____ other people.

COMPREHENSIVE UNDERSTANDING QUESTIONS

7-12min

07.   Give three examples of ways or actions by which Muslims harm other Muslims through their tongues.

DAY - 19

```
TEACHER NOTES / CORRECTIONS
```

7-12 min

08. Give three specific examples of people that Allaah has blessed you with in your life that you are grateful for.

TEACHER NOTES / CORRECTIONS

09. What are some possible ways that Muslims who are married can reflect their gratefulness to Allaah for their companion in life, in their interactions with their spouses and others?

7-12min

DAY - 19

TEACHER NOTES / CORRECTIONS

*[/3]=[/15]

TEST YOUR UNDERSTANDING:

TRUE & FALSE QUESTIONS

[Circle the correct letter for each individual sentence from today's content.]

3min

01. Permissible joking and innocent fun is acceptable in Islaam.   [T / F]

02. The Companions of the Messenger of Allaah, may Allaah be   [T / F]
pleased with them all, never smiled or joked with each other.

03. Simple amusement and fun between the Muslims can help get   [T / F]
rid of any hard feelings among them.

FILL IN THE BLANK QUESTIONS

[Enter the correct individual words to complete the sentences from today's content.]

6min

DAY - 20

04. It is permissible to _____ an individual to _____ due to what
they possess of _____ traits and _____ disposition.

05. It is from good character to speak _____ words and _____ in the
face of your _____ who visit you.

06. Innocent _____ is that which does not lead to anything _____.

COMPREHENSIVE UNDERSTANDING QUESTIONS

7-12 min

07. Give three examples of some permissible activities that the Muslims can do together to strengthen their good relations and brotherhood.

DAY - 20

```
TEACHER NOTES / CORRECTIONS
```

*[/ 3]

08. Give three additional examples that reflects a Muslim having good character with another Muslim.

DAY - 20

TEACHER NOTES / CORRECTIONS

09. Give three examples of things that Muslims could do to maintain harmony and good relations between themselves.

TEACHER NOTES / CORRECTIONS

*[/ 3]=[/ 15]

TEST YOUR UNDERSTANDING:

TRUE & FALSE QUESTIONS

[Circle the correct letter for each individual sentence from today's content.]

3 min

01. Muslims are rewarded for fulfilling those things which Allaah [T / F] has made obligatory upon them.

02. One will receive a reward from Allaah for buying things for the [T / F] members of his family regardless of the reason.

03. The disbelievers do not receive any good from the good that [T / F] they do to others, due to their disbelief in Islaam.

FILL IN THE BLANK QUESTIONS

[Enter the correct individual words to complete the sentences from today's content.]

6 min

DAY - 21

04. It is the _____ of Allaah in His creation that it is _____ for someone to undertake the specific _____ to achieve the _____ he seeks.

05. A Muslim receives a reward for everyone that eats from the _____ they earn with their _____ _____.

06. Whenever we eat or drink our _____ should be doing so upon the _____ of Allaah through _____ him.

COMPREHENSIVE UNDERSTANDING QUESTIONS

7-12min

07. Give an example of three possible acts which are means or tools to fulfill an obligation upon you as a Muslim.

DAY - 21

TEACHER NOTES / CORRECTIONS

*[/3]

7-12 min

08. Give an example of three possible things which could be purchased or acquired as tools to help us worship Allaah.

TEACHER NOTES / CORRECTIONS

09. What is another example of a rewarded obligation related to feeding people, which is connected to a pillar of Islaam?

TEACHER NOTES / CORRECTIONS

*[/ 3]=[/ 15]

TEST YOUR UNDERSTANDING:

TRUE & FALSE QUESTIONS

[Circle the correct letter for each individual sentence from today's content.]

3min

01. We can spend our money however we like, as long as it is spent [T / F] upon what is permissible.

02. One way of squandering or wasting your money is spending it [T / F] on things which are forbidden in Islaam.

03. A Muslim could be blameworthy in front of Allaah for refraining [T / F] to spend money on that which would benefit them and others.

FILL IN THE BLANK QUESTIONS

[Enter the correct individual words to complete the sentences from today's content.]

6min

DAY - 22

04. It is a _____ to spend your money on that which is from the spreading of _____ and _____.

05. A Muslim should spend his _____ only in that which is connected to the _____ of Allaah, or on _____ every day needs.

06. In _____ money you should be between _____, which is squandering your money away foolishly, and _____ which is being overly restrictive in what you spend.

COMPREHENSIVE UNDERSTANDING QUESTIONS

7-12min

07.   Give three possible examples of things which are permissible but which Muslims squander their money on.

DAY - 22

TEACHER NOTES / CORRECTIONS

✳[/ 3]

08. Give three possible examples of things that are prohibited and forbidden which Muslims squander their money on.

DAY - 22

TEACHER NOTES / CORRECTIONS

09. Give three possible examples of a Muslim spending their money moderately on matters considered related to the obedience of Allaah.

TEACHER NOTES / CORRECTIONS

*[/ 3]=[/ 15]

TEST YOUR UNDERSTANDING:

TRUE & FALSE QUESTIONS

[Circle the correct letter for each individual sentence from today's content.]

3min

01. There are many different legitimate ways to give charity in Islaam. [T / F]

02. If you cannot help someone financially, or help them in some other way of good service or assistance, then there are no other ways for you to give them charity. [T / F]

03. Bad feelings and unsupported abandonment between Muslims for personal reasons can cause tremendous harm and damage among the Muslims. [T / F]

FILL IN THE BLANK QUESTIONS

[Enter the correct individual words to complete the sentences from today's content.]

6 min

04. The Prophet, may the praise and salutations of Allaah be upon him, _____ his Ummah to _____ form of _____ that he knew of for them.

05. A Muslim should _____ seriously and strive _____ in doing righteous deeds.

06. The possible ways in which you can _____ _____ are numerous, just as the number of the parts of _____ _____ which Allaah has blessed you with are numerous.

DAY - 23

COMPREHENSIVE UNDERSTANDING QUESTIONS

7-12min

07.   Give three possible examples of ways of giving charity that people may easily overlook or not realize.

DAY - 23

TEACHER NOTES / CORRECTIONS

✳[/ 3]

08. What are some of the things that lead to personal differences and disputes among Muslims?

_____
_____
_____
_____
_____
_____
_____
_____
_____
_____
_____
_____
_____
_____
_____
_____
_____
_____
_____
_____
_____
_____
_____

DAY - 23

TEACHER NOTES / CORRECTIONS

_____
_____
_____
_____
_____

09. Why is it important that some of the people among the Muslims work to reconcile the personal problems and differences that occur among them?

DAY - 23

TEACHER NOTES / CORRECTIONS

*[/3]=[/15]

TEST YOUR UNDERSTANDING:

TRUE & FALSE QUESTIONS

[Circle the correct letter for each individual sentence from today's content.]

3 min

01. Dhikr only means the statements a Muslim makes a [T / F] certain number of times in remembrance of Allaah such as "subhanAllaah", "alhamdulillah", or "Allaahu akbar".

02. The right of good treatment of our neighbors includes many [T / F] different aspects and behaviors.

03. The studying of beneficial knowledge in Islaam is considered a [T / F] rewarded form of dhikr.

FILL IN THE BLANK QUESTIONS

[Enter the correct individual words to complete the sentences from today's content.]

6 min

04. It is obligatory upon you that you be _____ toward your guest by providing him _____, _____, and a place to _____.

05. The _____ of the tongue is that you generally restrict your tongue to that which brings you _____ or some _____.

06. It is _____ to respect the character of a Muslim, except when there is a stronger _____ justification which takes _____ over this.

DAY - 24

[/ 6]*

COMPREHENSIVE UNDERSTANDING QUESTIONS

7-12min

07.   Give examples of three possible forms of dhikr which Muslims may neglect or not take full advantage of.

_____

_____

_____

_____

_____

_____

_____

_____

_____

_____

_____

_____

_____

_____

_____

_____

_____

_____

_____

_____

_____

_____

DAY - 24

```
TEACHER NOTES / CORRECTIONS
```

_____

_____

_____

_____

✳[/3]

08. Give examples of three sinful types of speech engaged in by those who fail to imprison their tongues.

TEACHER NOTES / CORRECTIONS

09. Give an example where someone who is your neighbor, has other rights over you which are different than what another neighbor is due.

TEACHER NOTES / CORRECTIONS

*[/ 3]=[/ 15]

TEST YOUR UNDERSTANDING:

TRUE & FALSE QUESTIONS

[Circle the correct letter for each individual sentence from today's content.]

3min

01. If a Muslim sees something which is wrong, he should try to   [T / F] change or correct it in the proper way.

02. There is no problem with someone only focusing on indicating   [T / F] the mistakes and misguidance of others.

03. Speaking about the mistakes of other Muslims in their   [T / F] statements and actions is something that some people decided to focus on from their own selves and personal understanding.

FILL IN THE BLANK QUESTIONS

[Enter the correct individual words to complete the sentences from today's content.]

6min

04. Wrongdoing that we see among the Muslims should be _____ and _____ about by one speaking with good _____ and _____.

05. Both Muslim men and Muslim women must _____ to prevent themselves from following their _____ in_____ things.

06. The _____ establishment of the _____ punishments bring a general _____ for Muslim society as a whole.

DAY - 25

[/ 6]✳

COMPREHENSIVE UNDERSTANDING QUESTIONS

7-12 min

07.   What are some of the possible negative consequences of a Muslim neglecting his own shortcomings and focusing on the faults of other people?

_____

_____

_____

_____

_____

_____

_____

_____

_____

_____

_____

_____

_____

_____

_____

_____

_____

_____

_____

_____

_____

_____

_____

_____

_____

TEACHER NOTES / CORRECTIONS

DAY - 25

_____

_____

_____

_____

08. What are some of the possible negative consequences of some Muslims seeing some wrongdoing which they could advise the Muslims involved about, but instead only discuss among each other or whisper about it among themselves?

TEACHER NOTES / CORRECTIONS

09.   Give a general description of three affirmed set punishments found within the guidance of Islaam for specific transgressions within a Muslim society.

_____
_____
_____
_____
_____
_____
_____
_____
_____
_____
_____
_____
_____
_____
_____
_____
_____
_____
_____
_____
_____
_____
_____
_____

TEACHER NOTES / CORRECTIONS

_____
_____
_____
_____
_____

*[/3]=[/15]

TEST YOUR UNDERSTANDING:

TRUE & FALSE QUESTIONS

[Circle the correct letter for each individual sentence from today's content.]

3min

01. Offering the greeting of salaam to children is not something [T / F] which is important.

02. Teaching is an important form of giving charity in Islaam. [T / F]

03. It is important to do those permissible actions that facilitate [T / F] people accepting it when we offer them advice.

FILL IN THE BLANK QUESTIONS

[Enter the correct individual words to complete the sentences from today's content.]

6min

04. A Muslim should make an effort to _____ both the _____ and the _____ with greetings of salaam.

05. Young Muslims _____ from the _____ of those Muslims _____ than them.

06. Good _____ between older and younger Muslims, make it _____ for the older Muslims to _____ younger Muslims.

DAY - 26

COMPREHENSIVE UNDERSTANDING QUESTIONS

7-12min

07.   Why is it important to establish good relations in order to be able to give advice to others?

_____

_____

_____

_____

_____

_____

_____

_____

_____

_____

_____

_____

_____

_____

_____

_____

_____

_____

_____

_____

_____

_____

TEACHER NOTES / CORRECTIONS

DAY - 26

_____

_____

_____

_____

✳[/ 3]

7-12min

08.   Give three possible examples of things that younger Muslims do because of
       following the example of some older Muslims.

_____

_____

_____

_____

_____

_____

_____

_____

_____

_____

_____

_____

_____

_____

_____

_____

_____

_____

_____

_____

_____

_____

_____

TEACHER NOTES / CORRECTIONS

DAY - 26

_____

_____

_____

_____

_____

[/ 3]✴   *114*

09. Give any additional example of matters that the Companions of the Messenger of Allaah, may be pleased with them all, did and explained their reason for doing so was that they saw the Prophet himself do so.

7-12 min

_____

_____

_____

_____

_____

_____

_____

_____

_____

_____

_____

_____

_____

_____

_____

_____

_____

_____

_____

_____

_____

_____

_____

_____

_____

_____

_____

TEACHER NOTES / CORRECTIONS

DAY - 26

_____

_____

_____

_____

_____

✳[/ 3]=[/ 15]

TEST YOUR UNDERSTANDING:

TRUE & FALSE QUESTIONS

[Circle the correct letter for each individual sentence from today's content.]

3min

01. If the believer sees in his brother a shortcoming related to   [T / F]
something which is obligatory, he should just overlook it as we
all have shortcomings..

02. A Muslim is only responsible for recognizing faults in himself   [T / F]
and rectifying his own problems.

03. If someone commits a sin that leads to separation with his   [T / F]
brother, its source was something within himself.

FILL IN THE BLANK QUESTIONS

[Enter the correct individual words to complete the sentences from today's content.]

6min

04. _____ for the sake of Allaah between the Muslims produces _____
benefits and _____ benefits.

05. We must _____ our Muslim brother from whatever _____
and _____ that we can, whenever he is present with us or when
he is absent.

06. The Muslim who chooses to be _____ and not _____ his brother is
someone who does not understand the _____ of, and his _____
towards, his Muslim brothers and sisters.

DAY - 27

COMPREHENSIVE UNDERSTANDING QUESTIONS

7-12 min

07.   Give three possible examples of obligatory matters about which we should advise our Muslim brother or sister in a good way, if we know with certainty they were neglecting them.

_____

_____

_____

_____

_____

_____

_____

_____

_____

_____

_____

_____

_____

_____

_____

_____

_____

_____

_____

_____

TEACHER NOTES / CORRECTIONS

_____

_____

DAY - 27

_____

_____

_____

[/3]

08. Give three possible examples of prohibited matters about which we should advise our Muslim brother or sister in a good way, if we know with certainty that they had fallen into committing them.

_____

_____

_____

_____

_____

_____

_____

_____

_____

_____

_____

_____

_____

_____

_____

_____

_____

_____

_____

_____

_____

_____

_____

_____

_____

_____

_____

TEACHER NOTES / CORRECTIONS

DAY - 27

_____

_____

_____

_____

_____

[/ 3]✱

09. Give two possible examples of correctly protecting or defending your Muslim brother, one example when he would be present, and a second example of doing so when he would be absent.

7-12 min

TEACHER NOTES / CORRECTIONS

DAY - 27

*[/3]=[/15]

TEST YOUR UNDERSTANDING:

TRUE & FALSE QUESTIONS

[Circle the correct letter for each individual sentence from today's content.]

3 min

01. In relation to the mercy and forgiveness we put forth among   [T / F] Allaah's creation, we receive more mercy and forgiveness from Allaah.

02. It isn't dangerous to hear a reminder about a sin or transgression   [T / F] but not stop doing it right away.

03. The Messenger of Allaah, may the praise and salutations of   [T / F] Allaah be upon him, compared people who do not heed or hold onto that good advice and reminder given to them, to damaged or cracked containers.

FILL IN THE BLANK QUESTIONS

[Enter the correct individual words to complete the sentences from today's content.]

6 min

04. When you show _____ to others, _____ will show _____ to you.

05. The Messenger of Allaah, may the praise and salutations of Allaah be upon him, _____ the Muslims against being those who _____ an admonition or advice but fail to _____ it or fail to _____ it.

06. The _____ are those who seek _____ for the _____ and wrong that they do.

COMPREHENSIVE UNDERSTANDING QUESTIONS

7-12min

07.   Give three possible examples of admonitions which it is common for Muslims today to not pay much attention to.

_____

_____

_____

_____

_____

_____

_____

_____

_____

_____

_____

_____

_____

_____

_____

_____

_____

_____

_____

_____

TEACHER NOTES / CORRECTIONS

_____

_____

✳[/3]

7-12 min

08. What are some reasons why someone might persist in committing a sin, even after learning that it is wrong to do so?

_____
_____
_____
_____
_____
_____
_____
_____
_____
_____
_____
_____
_____
_____
_____
_____
_____
_____
_____
_____
_____
_____
_____
_____
_____

TEACHER NOTES / CORRECTIONS

_____
_____
_____
_____

DAY - 28

_____

[/ 3]✸

09. Give three possible examples of showing mercy to other Muslims in their affairs.

TEACHER NOTES / CORRECTIONS

*[/ 3]=[/ 15]

TEST YOUR UNDERSTANDING:

TRUE & FALSE QUESTIONS

[Circle the correct letter for each individual sentence from today's content.]

3min

01. Everything connected to our lives has been written down and   [T / F]
recorded by the Pen.

02. Since everything is decreed for us, there is no need to put forth   [T / F]
any effort to change or accomplish anything.

03. When someone seeks to obtain the expansion and increase   [T / F]
which was mentioned in these two hadeeth, it is something
outside of, or beyond, what has been decreed.

FILL IN THE BLANK QUESTIONS

[Enter the correct individual words to complete the sentences from today's content.]

6min

04. Every matter which is been written down will _____ according to its
recorded _____, _____, and _____.

05. The _____ of family ties is _____ according to the texts of the
Book of _____ and the authentic _____.

06. The _____ or _____ mentioned in these two hadeeth
means _____ _____ will be placed in the length of his life
or within his income.

DAY - 29

COMPREHENSIVE UNDERSTANDING QUESTIONS

7-12 min

07. Give two possible examples of things that you can do to maintain good family ties with distant relatives.

TEACHER NOTES / CORRECTIONS

DAY - 29

✱[/ 3]

7-12 min

08.   Give two possible examples of the results of Allah increasing the blessings in the income that you receive.

_____

_____

_____

_____

_____

_____

_____

_____

_____

_____

_____

_____

_____

_____

_____

_____

_____

_____

_____

_____

_____

_____

_____

TEACHER NOTES / CORRECTIONS

_____

_____

_____

_____

DAY - 29

[/ 3]✳

09. Give two possible examples of the results of Allah increasing the blessings in the decreed time of your lifespan.

TEACHER NOTES / CORRECTIONS

✳[/ 3]=[/ 15]

TEST YOUR UNDERSTANDING:

TRUE & FALSE QUESTIONS
[Circle the correct letter for each individual sentence from today's content.]

3 min

01. The most important objective someone should have today is establishing himself in society and contributing to its growth. [T / F]

02. Worshiping Allaah alone only refers to fulfilling those commands that we have been given. [T / F]

03. A general Muslim should sit with the people of knowledge to study the correct books which teach how to properly worship Allaah. [T / F]

FILL IN THE BLANK QUESTIONS
[Enter the correct individual words to complete the sentences from today's content.]

6 min

04. Every _____ responsible Muslim must direct every _____ of worship towards Allaah _____, excluding _____ or anything else.

05. Ritual _____ is the _____ form of _____ after one states the two testimonies of faith and has belief in Islaam.

06. The meaning of _____ the obligatory _____, is perform them in the correct way, _____ and _____.

COMPREHENSIVE UNDERSTANDING QUESTIONS

7-12 min

07. Give three additional examples of beliefs, statements, or actions which guide a Muslim towards the reward of Jannah, which have not been mentioned.

TEACHER NOTES / CORRECTIONS

DAY - 30

*[/3]

08. Give three examples of impermissible actions which are joining others with Allaah in the worship due to him alone.

TEACHER NOTES / CORRECTIONS

09.   Discuss any two established requirements related to performing the obligatory
ritual prayer correctly.

7-12 min

TEACHER NOTES / CORRECTIONS

DAY - 30

*[/ 3]=[/ 15]

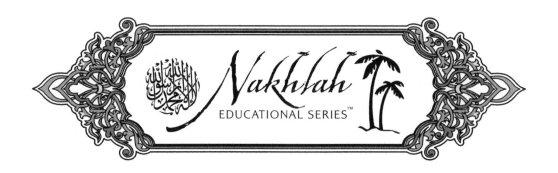

THE NAKHLAH EDUCATIONAL SERIES:

The Purpose of the 'Nakhlah Educational Series' is to contribute to the present knowledge based efforts which enable Muslim individuals, families, and communities to understand and learn Islaam and then to develop within and truly live Islaam. Our commitment and goal is to contribute beneficial publications and works that:

Firstly, reflect the priority, message and methodology of all the prophets and messengers sent to humanity, meaning that single revealed message which embodies the very purpose of life, and of human creation. As Allaah the Most High has said,

We sent a Messenger to every nation ordering them that they should worship Allaah alone, obey Him and make their worship purely for Him, and that they should avoid everything worshipped besides Allaah. So from them there were those whom Allaah guided to His religion, and there were those who were unbelievers for whom misguidance was ordained. So travel through the land and see the destruction that befell those who denied the Messengers and disbelieved.—(Surah an-Nahl: 36)

Sheikh Rabee'a ibn Haadee al-Madkhalee in his work entitled, '*The Methodology of the Prophets in Calling to Allaah, That is the Way of Wisdom and Intelligence.*' explains the essential, enduring message of all the prophets:

"*So what was the message which these noble, chosen men, may Allaah's praises and salutations of peace be upon them all, brought to their people? Indeed their mission encompassed every matter of good and distanced and restrained every matter of evil. They brought forth to mankind everything needed for their well-being and happiness in this world and the Hereafter. There is nothing good except that they guided the people towards it, and nothing evil except that they warned the people against it. ...*

This was the message found with all of the Messengers; that they should guide to every good and warn against every evil. However where did they start, what did they begin with and what did they concentrate upon? There are a number of essentials, basic principles, and fundamentals which all their calls were founded upon, and which were the starting point for calling the people to Allaah. These fundamental points and principles are: 1. The worship of Allaah alone without any associates 2. The sending of prophets to guide creation 3. The belief in the resurrection and the life of the Hereafter

These three principles are the area of commonality and unity within their calls, and stand as the fundamental principles which they were established upon. These principles are given the greatest importance in the Qur'aan and are fully explained in it. They are also its most important purpose upon which it centers and which it continually mentions. It further quotes intellectual and observable proofs for them in all its chapters as well as within most of its accounts of previous nations and given examples.

MISSION

This is known to those who have full understanding, and are able to consider carefully and comprehend well. All the Books revealed by Allaah have given great importance to these points and all of the various revealed laws of guidance are agreed upon them. And the most important and sublime of these three principles, and the most fundamental of them all is directing one's worship only towards Allaah alone, the Blessed and the Most High."

Today one finds that there are indeed many paths, groups, and organizations apparently presenting themselves as representing Islaam, which struggle to put forth an outwardly pleasing appearance to the general Muslims; but when their methods are placed upon the precise scale of conforming to priorities and methodology of the message of the prophets sent by Allaah, they can only be recognized as deficient paths- not simply in practice but in principle- leading not to success but rather only to inevitable failure. As Sheikh Saaleh al-Fauzaan, may Allaah preserve him, states in his introduction to the same above mentioned work on the methodology of all the prophets,

"So whichever call is not built upon these foundations, and whatever methodology is not from the methodology of the Messengers - then it will be frustrated and fail, and it will be effort and toil without any benefit. The clearest proofs of this are those present day groups and organizations which set out a methodology and program for themselves and their efforts of calling the people to Islaam which is different from the methodology of the Messengers. These groups have neglected the importance of the people having the correct belief and creed - except for a very few of them - and instead call for the correction of side-issues."

There can be no true success in any form for us as individuals, families, or larger communities without making the encompassing worship of Allaah alone, with no partners or associates, the very and only foundation of our lives. It is necessary that each individual knowingly choose to base his life upon that same foundation taught by all the prophets and messengers sent by the Lord of all the worlds, rather than simply delving into the assorted secondary concerns and issues invited to by the various numerous parties, innovated movements, and groups. Indeed Sheikh al-Albaanee, may Allaah have mercy upon him, stated:

"…We unreservedly combat against this way of having various different parties and groups. As this false way- of group or organizational allegiances - conforms to the statement of Allaah the Most High, ❖ **But they have broken their religion among them into sects, each group rejoicing in what is with it as its beliefs. And every party is pleased with whatever they stand with.** ❖*-(Surah al-Mu'minoon: 53) And in truth they are no separate groups and parties in Islaam itself. There is only one true party, as is stated in a verse in the Qur'an,* ❖ **Verily, it is the party of Allaah that will be the successful.** ❖*-(Surah al-Mujadilaah: 58). The party of Allaah are those people who stand with the Messenger of Allaah, may Allaah's praise and salutations be upon him, meaning that an individual proceeds upon the methodology of the Companions of the Messenger. Due to this we call for having sound knowledge of the Book and the Sunnah."*

(Knowledge Based Issues & Sharee'ah Rulings: The Rulings of The Guiding Scholar Sheikh Muhammad Naasiruddeen al-Albaanee Made in the City of Medina & In the Emirates – [Emiratee Fatwa no 114. P.30])

Secondly, building upon the above foundation, our commitment is to contributing publications and works which reflect the inherited message and methodology of the acknowledged scholars of the many various branches of Sharee'ah knowledge who stood upon the straight path of preserved guidance in every century and time since the time of our Messenger, may Allaah's praise and salutations be upon him. These people of knowledge, who are the inheritors of the Final Messenger, have always adhered closely to the two revealed sources of guidance: the Book of Allaah and the Sunnah of the Messenger of Allaah- may Allaah's praise and salutations be upon him, upon the united consensus, standing with the body of guided Muslims in every century - preserving and transmitting the true religion generation after generation. Indeed the Messenger of Allaah, may Allaah's praise and salutations be upon him, informed us that, *{ A group of people amongst my Ummah will remain obedient to Allaah's orders. They will not be harmed by those who leave them nor by those who oppose them, until Allaah's command for the Last Day comes upon them while they remain on the right path. }* (Authentically narrated in Saheeh al-Bukhaaree).

We live in an age in which the question frequently asked is, "*How do we make Islaam a reality?*" and perhaps the related and more fundamental question is, "*What is Islaam?*", such that innumerable different voices quickly stand to offer countless different conflicting answers through books, lectures, and every available form of modern media. Yet the only true course of properly understanding this question and its answer- for ourselves and our families -is to return to the criterion given to us by our beloved Messenger, may Allaah's praise and salutations be upon him. Indeed the Messenger of Allaah, may Allaah's praise and salutations be upon him, indicated in an authentic narration, clarifying the matter beyond doubt, that the only "Islaam" which enables one to be truly successful and saved in this world and the next is as he said, *{... that which I am upon and my Companions are upon today.}* (authentically narrated in Jaam'ea at-Tirmidhee) referring to that Islaam which stands upon unchanging revealed knowledge. While every other changed and altered form of Islaam, whether through some form of extremism or negligence, or through the addition or removal of something, regardless of whether that came from a good intention or an evil one- is not the religion that Allaah informed us abou when He revealed, *❝ This day, those who disbelieved have given up all hope of your religion; so fear them not, but fear Me. This day, I have perfected your religion for you, completed My Favor upon you, and have chosen for you Islaam as your religion.❞*–(Surah al-Maa'idah: 3)

The guiding scholar Sheikh al-Albaanee, may have mercy upon him, said,

"*...And specifically mentioning those among the callers who have taken upon themselves the guiding of the young Muslim generation upon Islaam, working to educate them with its education, and to socialize them with its culture. Yet they themselves have generally not attempted to unify their understanding of those matters about Islaam regarding which the people of Islaam today differ about so severely.*

MISSION

And the situation is certainly not as is falsely supposed by some individuals from among them who are heedless or negligent - that the differences that exist among them are only in secondary matters without entering into or affecting the fundamental issues or principles of the religion; and the examples to prove that this is not true are numerous and recognized by those who have studied the books of the many differing groups and sects, or by the one who has knowledge of the various differing concepts and beliefs held by the Muslims today."(Mukhtasir al-'Uloo Lil'Alee al-Ghafaar, page 55)

Similarly he, may Allaah have mercy upon him, explained:

"Indeed, Islaam is the only solution, and this statement is something which the various different Islamic groups, organizations, and movements could never disagree about. And this is something which is from the blessings of Allaah upon the Muslims. However there are significant differences between the different Islamic groups, organizations, and movements that are present today regarding that domain which working within will bring about our rectification. What is that area of work to endeavor within, striving to restore a way of life truly reflecting Islaam, renewing that system of living which comes from Islaam, and in order to establish the Islamic government? The groups and movements significantly differ upon this issue or point. Yet we hold that it is required to begin with the matters of tasfeeyah —clarification, and tarbeeyah -education and cultivation, with both of them being undertaken together.

As if we were to start with the issue of governing and politics, then it has been seen that those who occupy themselves with this focus firstly posses beliefs which are clearly corrupted and ruined, and secondly that their personal behavior, from the aspect of conforming to Islaam, is very far from conforming to the actual guidance of the Sharee'ah. While those who first concern themselves with working just to unite the people and gather the masses together under a broad banner of the general term "Islaam", then it is seen that within the minds of those speakers who raise such calls -in reality there is fact no actual clear understanding of what Islaam is. Moreover, the understanding they have of Islaam has no significant impact in starting to change and reform their own lives. Due to this reason you find that many such individuals from here and there, who hold this perspective, are unable to truly realize or reflect Islaam even in areas of their own personal lives in matters which it is in fact easily possible for them to implement. As he holds that no one - regardless of whether it is because of his arrogance or pridefulness - can enter into directing him in an area of his personal life!

Yet at the same time these same individuals are raising their voices saying, "Judgment is only for Allaah!" and "It is required that judgment of affairs be according to what Allaah revealed." And this is indeed a true statement. But the one who does not possess something certainly cannot give or offer it to others. The majority of Muslims today have not established the judgment of Allaah fully upon themselves, yet they still seek from others to establish the judgment of Allaah within their governments...

...And I understand that this issue or subject is not immune from there being those who oppose our methodology of tasfeeyah and tarbeeyah. As there is the one who would say, "But establishing this tasfeeyah and tarbeeyah is a matter which requires many long years!" So, I respond by saying, this is not an important consideration in this matter, what is important is that we carry out what we have been commanded to do within our religion and by our Mighty Lord. What is important is that we begin by properly understanding our religion first and foremost. After this is accomplished then it will not be important whether the road itself is long or short.

And indeed I direct this statement of mine towards those men who are callers to the religion among the Muslims, and towards the scholars and those who direct our affairs. I call for them to stand upon complete knowledge of true Islaam, and to fight against every form of negligence and heedlessness regarding the religion, and against differing and disputes, as Allaah has said, ◈...and do not dispute with one another for fear that you lose courage and your strength departs ◈—(Surah Al-Anfaal: 46).

(Quoted from the work, 'The Life of Sheikh al-Albaanee, His Influence in Present Day Fields of Sharee'ah Knowledge, & the Praise of the Scholars for Him.' volume 1 page 380-385)

The guiding scholar Sheikh Zayd al-Madkhalee, may Allaah protect him, stated in his writing, 'The Well Established Principles of the Way of the First Generations of Muslims: It's Enduring & Excellent Distinct Characteristics' that,

"From among these principles and characteristics is that the methodology of tasfeeyah -or clarification, and tarbeeyah -or education and cultivation- is clearly affirmed and established as a true way coming from the first three generations of Islaam, and is something well known to the people of true merit from among them, as is concluded by considering all the related evidence. What is intended by tasfeeyah, when referring to it generally, is clarifying that which is the truth from that which is falsehood, what is goodness from that which is harmful and corrupt, and when referring to its specific meanings it is distinguishing the noble Sunnah of the Prophet and the people of the Sunnah from those innovated matters brought into the religion and the people who are supporters of such innovations.

As for what is intended by tarbeeyah, it is calling all of the creation to take on the manners and embrace the excellent character invited to by that guidance revealed to them by their Lord through His worshiper and Messenger Muhammad, may Allaah's praise and salutations be upon him; so that they might have good character, manners, and behavior. As without this they cannot have a good life, nor can they put right their present condition or their final destination. And we seek refuge in Allaah from the evil of not being able to achieve that rectification."

Thus the methodology of the people of standing upon the Prophet's Sunnah, and proceeding upon the 'way of the believers' in every century is reflected in a focus and concern with these two essential matters: tasfeeyah or clarification of what is original, revealed message from the Lord of all the worlds, and tarbeeyah or education and raising of ourselves, our families, and our communities, and our lands upon what has been distinguished to be that true message and path.

MISSION

The Roles of the Scholars & General Muslims In Raising the New Generation

The priority and focus of the 'Nakhlah Educational Series' is reflected within in the following statements of Sheikh al-Albaanee, may Allaah have mercy upon him:

"As for the other obligation, then I intend by this the education of the young generation upon Islaam purified from all of those impurities we have mentioned, giving them a correct Islamic education from their very earliest years, without any influence of a foreign, disbelieving education."

(Silsilat al-Hadeeth ad-Da'eefah, Introduction page 2.)

"...And since the Messenger of Allaah, may Allaah's praise and salutations be upon him, has indicated that the only cure to remove this state of humiliation that we find ourselves entrenched within, is truly returning back to the religion. Then it is clearly obligatory upon us - through the people of knowledge- to correctly and properly understand the religion in a way that conforms to the sources of the Book of Allaah and the Sunnah, and that we educate and raise a new virtuous, righteous generation upon this."

(Clarification and Cultivation and the Need of the Muslims for Them)

It is essential in discussing our perspective upon this obligation of raising the new generation of Muslims, that we highlight and bring attention to a required pillar of these efforts as indicated by Sheikh al-Albaanee, may Allaah have mercy upon him, and others- in the golden words, *"through the people of knowledge"*. Since something we commonly experience today is that many people have various incorrect understandings of the role that the scholars should have in the life of a Muslim, failing to understand the way in which they fulfill their position as the inheritors of the Messenger of Allaah, may Allaah's praise and salutations be upon him, and stand as those who preserve and enable us to practice the guidance of Islaam. Indeed, the noble Imaam Sheikh as-Sa'dee, may Allaah have mercy upon him, in his work, *"A Definitive and Clear Explanation of the Work 'A Triumph for the Saved Sect'"* pages 237-240, has explained this crucial issue with an extraordinary explanation full of remarkable benefits:

"Section: Explaining the Conditions for These Two Source Texts to Suffice You -or the Finding of Sufficiency in these Two Sources of Revelation.

Overall the conditions needed to achieve this and bring it about return to two matters:

Firstly, the presence of the requirements necessary for achieving this; meaning a complete devotion to the Book and the Sunnah, and the putting forth of efforts both in seeking to understand their intended meanings, as well as in striving to be guided by them. What is required secondly is the pushing away of everything which prevents achieving this finding of sufficiency in them.

This is through having a firm determination to distance yourself from everything which contradicts these two source texts in what comes from the historical schools of jurisprudence, assorted various statements, differing principles and their resulting conclusions which the majority of people proceed upon. These matters which contradict the two sources of revelation include many affairs which, when the worshiper of Allaah repels them from himself and stands against them, the realm of his knowledge, understanding, and deeds then expands greatly. Through a devotion to them and a complete dedication towards these two sources of revelation, proceeding upon every path which assists one's understanding them, and receiving enlightenment from the light of the scholars and being guided by the guidance that they possess- you will achieve that complete sufficiency in them. And surely, in the positions they take towards the leading people of knowledge and the scholars, the people are three types of individuals:

The first of them is the one who goes to extremes in his attachment to the scholars. He makes their statements something which are infallible as if their words held the same position as those of the statements of the Messenger of Allaah, may Allaah's praise and salutations be upon him, as well as giving those scholars' statements precedence and predominance over the Book of Allaah and the Sunnah. This is despite the fact that every leading scholar who has been accepted by this Ummah was one who promoted and encouraged the following of the Book and the Sunnah, commanding the people not to follow their own statements nor their school of thought in anything which stood in opposition to the Book of Allaah and the Sunnah.

The second type is the one who generally rejects and invalidates the statements of the scholars and forbids the referring to the statements of the leading scholars of guidance and those people of knowledge who stand as brilliant lamps in the darkness. This type of person neither relies upon the light of discernment with the scholars, nor utilizes their stores of knowledge. Or even if perhaps they do so, they do not direct thanks towards them for this. And this manner and way prohibits them from tremendous good. Furthermore, that which motivates such individuals to proceed in this way is their falsely supposing that the obligation to follow the Messenger of Allaah, may Allaah's praise and salutations be upon him, and the giving of precedence to his statements over the statements of anyone else, requires that they do without any reliance upon the statements of the Companions, or those who followed them in goodness, or those leading scholars of guidance within the Ummah. And this is a glaring and extraordinary mistake.

As indeed the Companions and the people of knowledge are the means and the agency between the Messenger of Allaah, may Allaah's praise and salutations be upon him, and his Ummah- in the transmission and spreading his Sunnah in regard to both its wording and texts as well as its meanings and understanding. Therefore the one who follows them in what they convey in this is guided through their understandings, receives knowledge from the light they possess, benefits from the conclusions they have derived from these sources -of beneficial meanings and explanations, as well as in relation to subtle matters which scarcely occur to the minds of some of the other people of knowledge, or barely comes to be discerned by their minds. Consequently, from the blessing of Allaah upon this Ummah is that He has given them these guiding scholars who cultivate and educate them upon two clear types of excellent cultivation.

The first category is education from the direction of ones knowledge and understanding. They educate the Ummah upon the more essential and fundamental matters before the more complex affairs. They convey the meanings of the Book and the Sunnah to the minds and intellects of the people through efforts of teaching which rectifies, and through composing various beneficial books of knowledge which a worshiper doesn't even have the ability to adequately describe what is encompassed within them of aspects of knowledge and benefits. Works which reflect the presence of a clear white hand in deriving guidance from the Book of Allaah and the Sunnah, and through the arrangement, detailed clarification, division and explanation, through the gathering together of explanations, comparisons, conditions, pillars, and explanations about that which prevents the fulfillment of matters, as well as distinguishing between differing meanings and categorizing various knowledge based benefits.

The second category is education from the direction of ones conduct and actions. They cultivate the peoples characters encouraging them towards every praiseworthy aspect of good character, through explaining its ruling and high status, and what benefits comes to be realized from it, clarifying the reasons and paths which enable one to attain it, as well as those affairs which prevent, delay or hinder someone becoming one distinguished and characterized by it. Because they, in reality, are those who bring nourishment to the hearts and the souls; they are the doctors who treat the diseases of the heart and its defects. As such they educate the people through their statements, actions as well as their general guided way. Therefore the scholars have a tremendous right over this Ummah. The portion of love and esteem, respect and honor, and thanks due to them because their merits and their various good efforts stand above every other right after establishing the right of Allaah, and the right of His Messenger, may Allaah's praise and salutations be upon him.

Because of this, the third group of individuals in respect to the scholars are those who have been guided to understand their true role and position, and establish their rights, thanking them for their virtues and merits, benefiting by taking from the knowledge they have, while acknowledging their rank and status. They understand that the scholars are not infallible and that their statements must stand in conformance to the statements of the Messenger of Allaah, may Allaah's praise and salutations be upon him. And that each one from among them has that which is from guidance, knowledge, and correctness in his statements taken and benefited from, while turning away from whatever in mistaken within it.

Yet such a scholar is not to be belittled for his mistake, as he stands as one who strove to reach the truth; therefore his mistake will be forgiven, and he should be thanked for his efforts. One clarifies what was stated by of any one of these leaders from among men, when it is recognizes that it has some weakness or conflict to an evidence of the Sharee'ah, by explaining its weakness and the level of that weakness, without speaking evilly of the intention of those people of knowledge and religion, nor defaming them due to that error. Rather we say, as it is obligatory to say, "And those who came after them say: ❦ **Our Lord! forgive us and our brethren who have preceded us in faith, and put not in our hearts any hatred against those who have believed. Our Lord! You are indeed full of kindness, Most Merciful.** ❦ -(Surah al-Hashr: 10).

Accordingly, individuals of this third type are those who fulfill two different matters. They join together on one hand between giving precedence to the Book and the Sunnah over everything else, and, on the other hand, between comprehending the level and position of the scholars and the leading people of knowledge and guidance, and establishing this even if it is only done in regard to some of their rights upon us. So we ask Allaah to bless us to be from this type, and to make us from among the people of this third type, and to make us from those who love Him and love those who love Him, and those who love every action which brings us closer to everything He loves."

Upon this clarity regarding the proper understanding of our balanced position towards our guided Muslim scholars, consider the following words about the realm of work of the general people of faith, which explains our area of efforts and struggle as Muslim parents, found in the following statement by Sheikh Saaleh Fauzaan al-Fauzaan, may Allaah preserve him.

"Question: Some people mistakenly believe that calling to Allaah is a matter not to be undertaken by anyone else other than the scholars without exception, and that it is not something required for other than the scholars according to that which they have knowledge of -to undertake any efforts of calling the people to Allaah. So what is your esteemed guidance regarding this?" The Sheikh responded by saying:

"This is not a misconception, but is in fact a reality. The call to Allaah cannot be established except through those who are scholars. And I state this. Yet, certainly there are clear issues which every person understands. As such, every individual should enjoin the good and forbid wrongdoing according to the level of his understanding. Such that he instructs and orders the members of his household to perform the ritual daily prayers and other matters that are clear and well known.

*Undertaking this is something mandatory and required even upon the common people, such that they must command their children to perform their prayers in the masjid. The Messenger of Allaah, may Allaah praise and salutations be upon him, said, { **Command you children to pray at seven, and beat them due to its negligence at ten.**} (Authentic narration found in Sunan Abu Dawood). And the Messenger of Allaah, may Allaah praise and salutations be upon him, said, { **Each one of you is a guardian or a shepherd, and each of you is responsible for those under his guardianship....**} (Authentic narration found in Saheeh al-Bukhaaree). So this is called guardianship, and this is also called enjoining the good and forbidding wrongdoing. The Messenger of Allaah, may Allaah praise and salutations be upon him, said, { **The one from among you who sees a wrong should change it with his hand, and if he is unable to do so, then with his tongue, and if he is not able to do this, then with his heart.** } (Authentic narration found in Saheeh Muslim).*

So in relation to the common person, that which it is required from him to endeavor upon is that he commands the members of his household-as well as others -with the proper performance of the ritual prayers, the obligatory charity, with generally striving to obey Allaah, and to stay away from sins and transgressions, and that he purify and cleanse his home from disobedience, and that he educate and cultivate his children upon the obedience of Allaah's commands. This is what is required from him, even if he is a general person. As these types of matters are from that which is understood by every single person. This is something which is clear and apparent.

MISSION

But as for the matters of putting forth rulings and judgments regarding matters in the religion, or entering into clarifying issues of what is permissible and what is forbidden, or explaining what is considered associating others in the worship due to Allaah and what is properly worshiping Him alone without any partner- then indeed these are matters which cannot be established except by the scholars"

(Beneficial Responses to Questions About Modern Methodologies, Question 15, page 22)

Similarly the guiding scholar Sheikh 'Abdul-'Azeez Ibn Baaz, may Allaah have mercy upon him, also emphasized this same overall responsibility:

"...It is also upon a Muslim that he struggles diligently in that which will place his worldly affairs in a good state, just as he must also strive in the correcting of his religious affairs and the affairs of his own family. As the people of his household have a significant right over him that he strive diligently in rectifying their affair and guiding them towards goodness, due to the statement of Allaah, the Most Exalted, ﴾ **Oh you who believe! Save yourselves and your families Hellfire whose fuel is men and stones** ﴿ *-(Surah at-Tahreem: 6)*

So it is upon you to strive to correct the affairs of the members of your family. This includes your wife, your children- both male and female- and such as your own brothers. This concerns all of the people in your family, meaning you should strive to teach them the religion, guiding and directing them, and warning them from those matters Allaah has prohibited for us. Because you are the one who is responsible for them as shown in the statement of the Prophet, may Allaah's praise and salutations be upon him, { **Every one of you is a guardian, and responsible for what is in his custody. The ruler is a guardian of his subjects and responsible for them; a husband is a guardian of his family and is responsible for it; a lady is a guardian of her husband's house and is responsible for it, and a servant is a guardian of his master's property and is responsible for it....**} *Then the Messenger of Allaah, may Allaah's praise and salutations be upon him, continued to say,* {**...so all of you are guardians and are responsible for those under your authority.**} *(Authentically narrated in Saheeh al-Bukhaaree & Muslim)*

It is upon us to strive diligently in correcting the affairs of the members of our families, from the aspect of purifying their sincerity of intention for Allaah's sake alone in all of their deeds, and ensuring that they truthfully believe in and follow the Messenger of Allaah, may Allaah's praise and salutations be upon him, their fulfilling the prayer and the other obligations which Allaah the Most Exalted has commanded for us, as well as from the direction of distancing them from everything which Allaah has prohibited.

It is upon every single man and women to give advice to their families about the fulfillment of what is obligatory upon them. Certainly, it is upon the woman as well as upon the man to perform this. In this way our homes become corrected and rectified in regard to the most important and essential matters. Allaah said to His Prophet, may Allaah's praise and salutations be upon him, ﴾ **And enjoin the ritual prayers on your family...** ﴿ *(Surah Taha: 132) Similarly, Allaah the Most Exalted said to His prophet Ismaa'aeel,* ﴾ **And mention in the Book, Ismaa'aeel. Verily, he was true to what he promised, and he was a Messenger, and a Prophet. And he used to enjoin on his family and his people the ritual prayers and the obligatory charity, and his Lord was pleased with him.** ﴿ *-(Surah Maryam: 54-55)*

As such, it is only proper that we model ourselves after the prophets and the best of people, and be concerned with the state of the members of our households. Do not be neglectful of them, oh worshipper of Allaah! Regardless of whether it is concerning your wife, your mother, father, grandfather, grandmother, your brothers, or your children; it is upon you to strive diligently in correcting their state and condition..."

(Collection of Various Rulings and Statements- Sheikh 'Abdul-'Azeez Ibn 'Abdullah Ibn Baaz, Vol. 6, page 47)

CONTENT & STRUCTURE:

We hope to contribute works which enable every striving Muslim who acknowledges the proper position of the scholars, to fulfill the recognized duty and obligation which lays upon each one of us to bring the light of Islaam into our own lives as individuals as well as into our homes and among our families. Towards this goal we are committed to developing educational publications and comprehensive educational curricula -through cooperation with and based upon the works of the scholars of Islaam and the students of knowledge. Works which, with the assistance of Allaah, the Most High, we can utilize to educate and instruct ourselves, our families and our communities upon Islaam in both principle and practice. The publications and works of the Nakhlah Educational Series are divided into the following categories:

Basic / Elementary: Ages 4-11
Secondary: Ages 11-14
High School: Ages 14- Young Adult
General: Young Adult –Adult
Supplementary: All Ages

Publications and works within these stated levels will, with the permission of Allaah, encompass different beneficial areas and subjects, and will be offered in every permissible form of media and medium. As certainly, as the guiding scholar Sheikh Saaleh Fauzaan al-Fauzaan, may Allaah preserve him, has stated,

"Beneficial knowledge is itself divided into two categories. Firstly is that knowledge which is tremendous in its benefit, as it benefits in this world and continues to benefit in the Hereafter. This is religious Sharee'ah knowledge. And secondly, that which is limited and restricted to matters related to the life of this world, such as learning the processes of manufacturing various goods. This is a category of knowledge related specifically to worldly affairs.

...As for the learning of worldly knowledge, such as knowledge of manufacturing, then it is legislated upon us collectively to learn whatever the Muslims have a need for. Yet, if they do not have a need for this knowledge, then learning it is a neutral matter upon the condition that it does not compete with or displace any areas of Sharee'ah knowledge..."

("Explanations of the Mistakes of Some Writers", Pages 10-12)

So we strive always to remind ourselves and our brothers of this crucial point also indicated by Sheikh Sadeeq Ibn Hasan al-Qanoojee, may Allaah have mercy upon him, in: *'Abjad al-'Uloom'*, (page 89)

MISSION

"...What is intended by knowledge in the mentioned hadeeth is knowledge of the religion and the distinctive Sharee'ah, knowledge of the Noble Book and the pure Sunnah, of which there is no third along with them. But what is not meant in this narration are those invented areas of knowledge, whether they emerged in previous ages or today's world, which the people in these present times have devoted themselves to. They have specifically dedicated themselves to them in a manner which prevents them from looking towards those areas of knowledge related to faith, and in a way which has preoccupied them from occupying themselves from what is actually wanted or desired by Allaah, the Most High, and His Messenger, who is the leader of men and Jinn. Such that the knowledge in the Qur'aan has become something abandoned and the sciences of hadeeth have become obscure. While these new areas of knowledge related to manufacturing and production continually emerge from the nations of disbelief and apostasy, and they are called, "sciences", "arts", and "ideal development". And this sad state increases every day, indeed from Allaah we came and to Him shall we return....

...Additionally, although the various areas of beneficial knowledge all share some level of value, they all have differing importance and ranks. Among them is that which is to be considered according to its subject, such as medicine, and its subject is the human body. Or such as the sciences of 'tafseer' and its subject is the explanation of the words of Allaah, the Most Exalted and Most High, and the value of these two areas is not in any way unrecognized.

And from among the various areas there are those areas which are considered according to their objective, such as knowledge of upright character, and its goal is understanding the beneficial merits that an individual can come to possess. And from among them there are those areas which are considered according to the people's need for them, such as 'fiqh' which the need for it is urgent and essential. And from among them there are those areas which are considered according to their apparent strength, such as knowledge of physical sports and exercise, as it is something openly demonstrated.

And from the areas of knowledge are those areas which rise in their position of importance through their combining all these different matters within them, or the majority of them. Such as revealed religious knowledge, as its subject is indeed esteemed, its objective one of true merit, and its need is undeniably felt. Likewise one area of knowledge may be considered of superior rank than another in consideration of the results that it brings forth, or the strength of its outward manifestation, or due to the essentialness of its objective. Similarly the result that an area produces is certainly of higher estimation and significance in appraisal than the outward or apparent significance of some other areas of knowledge.

For that reason the highest ranking and most valuable area of knowledge is that of knowledge of Allaah the Most Perfect and the Most High, of His angels, and messengers, and all the particulars of these beliefs, as its result is that of eternal and continuing happiness."

We ask Allaah, the most High to bless us with success in contributing to the many efforts of our Muslim brothers and sisters committed to raising themselves as individuals and the next generation of our children upon that Islaam which Allaah has perfected and chosen for us, and which He has enabled the guided Muslims to proceed upon in each and every century. We ask him to forgive us, and forgive the Muslim men and the Muslim women, and to guide all the believers to everything He loves and is pleased with. The success is from Allaah, The Most High The Most Exalted, alone and all praise is due to Him.

Abu Sukhailah Khalil Ibn-Abelahyi
Taalib al-Ilm Educational Resources

GENERAL ANNOUNCEMENT:

Taalib al-Ilm Educational Publications is looking for

Distributors:

We are working to make Taalib al-Ilm Education Resources publications available through distributors worldwide. Our present discounts for wholesalers are:

50% discount for any order of **USD** **$2000** or over retail cost

60% discount for any order of **USD** **$5000** or over retail cost

For further information, please contact the sales department by e-mail: *service@taalib.com.*

Publication Contributors:

Additionally, in an effort to further expand our publication library, we are seeking contributing authors, translators, and compilers with beneficial works of any area of Sharee'ah knowledge for submission of their works for potential publication by us. For details and all submission guidelines please email us at: *service@taalib.com*

Referral bonus: *Individuals who refer a new distributor or publication contributor to us can receive a **$25 PayPal payment** upon:*

1) a confirmed contract with a publication contributor or

2) receipt of a newly referred distributor's initial order at the 50% discount level.

Contact us for further information and conditions.

MISSION

30 Days of Guidance:
Learning Fundamental Principles of Islaam

A Short Journey Within the Work al-Ibanah al-Sughrah With
Sheikh 'Abdul-Azeez Ibn 'Abdullah ar-Raajhee
(may Allaah preserve him)

The role of Islaam in today's world is something, which is indisputable and often contested. Yet people have different understandings of Islaam which range from dangerous extremism, which distorts the religion, all the way to vulnerable laxity, which nullifies many of the authentic beliefs and practices of revealed guidance. As such, it is a blessing for Muslims today that our well-known scholars continue to work diligently in examining openly and clarifying the false ideas and practices that are attributed to Islaam by both non-Muslims and by Muslims themselves.

This work approaches the challenge of learning important fundamentals in a way that allows an individual to proceed through discussions related to them a day at a time over thirty day,s, all based upon the explanations of one of today's noble guiding scholars. This book also includes seven essential appendices that cover important issues and guidance related to weighing and assessing the many of claims of what is "Islamic" today.

Compiled and Translated by:
Abu Sukhailah Khalil Ibn-Abelahyi

[Available: **Now** ¦ price: **(SS) $27.50 (DS) $25 (W) $12** ¦ **(Kindle) $9.99**]

An Educational Course Based Upon:

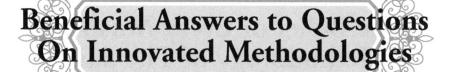

Beneficial Answers to Questions On Innovated Methodologies

By the Guiding Scholar
Sheikh Saaleh Ibn Abdullah al-Fauzaan
(may Allaah preserve him)

This course focuses upon the importance of clarity in the way you understand and practice Islaam, in the midst of today's confusing claims to Islaam.
What is the right way or methodology, to practice Islaam? Examine evidences and proofs from the sources texts of the Qur'aan and Sunnah along with the statements of many scholars explaining them, which connect you directly to that Islaam which the Messenger of Allaah ﷺ taught his Companions, may Allaah be pleased with them all.

Course Features:
Twenty concise illustrated lessons to facilitate learning & review with several important textual & course appendices.

Compiled and Translated by:
Abu Sukhailah Khalil Ibn-Abelahyi

[Available: **Now** ¦ price: (SS) $35 (DS) $32.50
(W) $12 ¦ (Kindle) $9.99]

PREVIEW

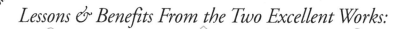

Lessons & Benefits From the Two Excellent Works:

The Belief of Every Muslim &
The Methodology of The Saved Sect

By the Guiding Scholar
Sheikh Muhammad Ibn Jameel Zaynoo
(may Allaah preserve him)

This course begins with three full lessons with specific practical guidelines on how to effectively study Islaam and gain the knowledge needed to build your life as a Muslim into a life which is pleasing to Allaah.

Through twenty lessons on knowledge, beliefs, & methodology along with quizzes, review questions & lesson benefits -the remaining lessons take simply explained passages from two beneficial works that cover many important principles and the common misconceptions connected to them, which are fundamental to correctly understanding Islaam as it was taught to the Companions of the Messenger of Allaah.

Compiled and Translated by:

Abu Sukhailah Khalil Ibn-Abelahyi

[Available: **Now** ¦ price: **(SS) $27.50 (DS) $25
(W) $12** ¦ **(Kindle) $9.99**]

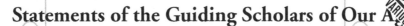

Statements of the Guiding Scholars of Our Age

Regarding Books & their Advice to the Beginner Seeker of Knowledge

with Selections from the Following Scholars:

Sheikh 'Abdul-'Azeez ibn 'Abdullah ibn Baaz -Sheikh Muhammad ibn Saaleh al-'Utheimein - Sheikh Muhammad Naasiruddeen al-Albaanee - Sheikh Muqbil ibn Haadee al-Waada'ee - Sheikh 'Abdur-Rahman ibn Naaser as-Sa'adee - Sheikh Muhammad 'Amaan al-Jaamee - Sheikh Muhammad al-Ameen as-Shanqeetee - Sheikh Ahmad ibn Yahya an-Najmee
(May Allaah have mercy upon them)

Sheikh Saaleh al-Fauzaan ibn 'Abdullah al-Fauzaan - Sheikh Saaleh ibn 'Abdul-'Azeez Aal-Sheikh - Sheikh Muhammad ibn 'Abdul-Wahhab al-Wasaabee -Permanent Committee to Scholastic Research & Issuing Of Islamic Rulings
(May Allaah preserve them.)

Book Sections:

1. Guidance and Direction for Every Male and Female Muslim

2. Golden Advice that Benefits the Beginner Regarding Acquiring Knowledge

3. Beneficial Guidance for Female Students of Sharee'ah Knowledge

4 Guidance from the Scholars Regarding Important Books to Acquire for Seeking Knowledge

5. The Warning of the Scholars from the Books of those who have Deviated &
the Means and Ways of Going Astray

6. Clear Statements from the Scholars' Advice Regarding Memorizing Knowledge

7. Issues Related to the Verifiers of Books in our Age

Compiled and Translated by:
Abu Sukhailah Khalil Ibn-Abelahyi

[Available: **Now** ¦ price: **(HB) $32.50 (SB) $25**
¦ **(Kindle) $9.99**]

Whispers of Paradise (1):

A Muslim Woman's Life Journal

An Islamic Daily Journal Which Encourages Reflection & Rectification

Abu Alee ath-Thaqafee said: Abu Hafs used to say:
"The one who does not each moment weigh his situation
and condition against the scale of the Book of Allaah and
the Sunnah, and does not question his very footsteps,
then he is not to be considered worthy."
(Seyaar 'Alaam an-Nubala: vol. 12, page 512)

12 Monthly calendar pages with beneficial quotations
from Ibn Qayyim & *Daily journal page* based upon
Hijree calendar(with corresponding C.E. dates)

Each daily journal page starts with one of the following:

-A Verse from the Noble Qur'aan
-An Authentic Narration of the Messenger of Allaah
-An Authentic Supplication
-A Beneficial Point from a Biography of the
Early Generations
-A Beneficial Statement from One of the
Well Known Scholars, Past or Present

Available: **Now** | price: **$25**
[New elegantly designed edition for each year]

PREVIEW

Made in United States
North Haven, CT
21 April 2022